Reigniting Employee Engagement

Tom Atchison

Reigniting Employee Engagement

A Guide to Rediscovering Purpose and Meaning in Healthcare

ACHE Management Series

Your board, staff, or clients may also benefit from this book's insight. For information on quantity discounts, contact the Health Administration Press Marketing Manager at (312) 424-9450.

This publication is intended to provide accurate and authoritative information in regard to the subject matter covered. It is sold, or otherwise provided, with the understanding that the publisher is not engaged in rendering professional services. If professional advice or other expert assistance is required, the services of a competent professional should be sought.

The statements and opinions contained in this book are strictly those of the author and do not represent the official positions of the American College of Healthcare Executives or the Foundation of the American College of Healthcare Executives.

26   25   24   23   22   5   4   3   2

Library of Congress Cataloging-in-Publication Data

Names: Atchison, Thomas A., 1945– author. | American College of Healthcare Executives
   issuing body.
Title: Reigniting employee engagement : a guide to rediscovering purpose and meaning in
   healthcare / Tom Atchison.
Other titles: Management series (Ann Arbor, Mich.)
Description: Chicago, IL : Health Administration Press, [2022] | Series: HAP/ACHE
   management series | Includes bibliographical references and index. | Summary: "Rising
   caregiver burnout is a critical issue, and this book presents a simple model for reenergizing the
   healthcare workforce and creating sustainable employee engagement by refocusing on basic
   human needs"—Provided by publisher.
Identifiers: LCCN 2021030754 (print) | LCCN 2021030755 (ebook) | ISBN 9781640552975
   (paperback ; alk. paper) | ISBN 9781640552944 (epub)
Subjects: MESH: Health Services Administration | Work Engagement | Organizational Culture
Classification: LCC RA971 (print) | LCC RA971 (ebook) | NLM W 84.1 | DDC
   362.1068—dc23
LC record available at https://lccn.loc.gov/2021030754
LC ebook record available at https://lccn.loc.gov/2021030755

The paper used in this publication meets the minimum requirements of American National Standard for Information Sciences—Permanence of Paper for Printed Library Materials, ANSI Z39.48-1984. ∞™

Acquisitions editor: Jennette McClain; Manuscript editor: Deborah Ring; Project manager: Andrew Baumann; Cover design: James Slate; Layout: Integra

Found an error or a typo? We want to know! Please e-mail it to hapbooks@ache.org, mentioning the book's title and putting "Book Error" in the subject line.

For photocopying and copyright information, please contact Copyright Clearance Center at www.copyright.com or at (978) 750-8400.

Health Administration Press
A division of the Foundation of the American
   College of Healthcare Executives
300 S. Riverside Plaza, Suite 1900
Chicago, IL 60606-6698
(312) 424-2800

Contents

Preface

WHY WRITE A book about finding meaning and purpose while working in the healthcare industry? The past three or four decades have seen a dramatic shift in the ethos of working in healthcare, especially for physicians and other caregivers. An internist friend of mine recently told me that he had always believed that he was called to be a physician. That calling required him to do everything he could for his patients. But over the last several years, the meaning, purpose, and joy that he found in his calling had diminished greatly. His daily work was less about patient care and more about being a "pieceworker." He reported that it had been a long time since an executive had asked him about his patients. The most common question he heard from administration was "Did you hit your numbers today?"

What happened to erode the personal meaning, joy, pride, and purpose of being a caregiver? This book attempts to answer that question and provides a toolkit for those working in healthcare to begin to rekindle personal and professional meaning and purpose.

Parts of this book may be hard to read, and even to accept. The data on burnout, preventable deaths, and the roles of corporate medicine, government, and the insurance industry make clear why caregivers are struggling to find meaning in their work. The corporate culture in today's healthcare industry conspires to deaden the human soul. It is my hope that by sharing data on these factors in this book, I can help healthcare leaders see the importance of creating a culture that instead *feeds* the human soul.

Working in healthcare is hard. And it is getting harder. Dozens of articles have been written about burnout, which the Cleveland Clinic defines as "a state of physical, emotional and mental exhaustion" that may cause caregivers to experience "fatigue, anxiety, and depression." Just about everyone who works in healthcare today is experiencing more disengagement and feeling more like "economic units" than professional caregivers. Many high-level executives, physicians, nurses, and other healthcare professionals can easily recite the number of years, months, and days until they can retire! The healthcare profession—caring for others at a difficult time in their lives—was once a calling. Now, it seems that working in healthcare is just a job.

The popular antidote to burnout is resilience. Countless books, articles, and seminars are devoted to increasing individual and organizational resilience. However, as the famous management consultant W. Edwards Deming told us, "A bad system will beat a good person every time." In many ways, the current healthcare system in the United States is a bad system that is beating some very good people!

The story of the boiling frog is a good analogy that illustrates why resilience training is an incomplete solution to the problem of burnout. According to this oft-told tale, if you put a frog into a pot of boiling water, it will immediately jump out. But if you put a frog into a pot of room-temperature water and gradually bring the temperature up to boiling, the frog won't even realize that it is being boiled alive. Responding to chronic burnout with resilience training is like helping the frog learn to enjoy the hot water. Resilience training does not address the root cause of burnout, which is workers' loss of meaning and inability to find purpose in the healthcare industry. The essential question is, What personal, interpersonal, structural, or process dynamics are *causing* this loss of meaning and purpose?

The inspiration for this text was Deming's statement quoted earlier. Too many good people are no longer able to find meaning in their work in healthcare. Increasing regulatory requirements, financial pressures, and constant pressure to improve quality while reducing costs: The sum of these increasing extraordinary pressures is a disengaged healthcare workforce.

A highly skilled, intelligent, and patient-focused physician whom I have known for more than a decade recently sent a letter to all her patients. The first two paragraphs read as follows:

Dear Patient,

It has been a great pleasure to work with you, and I have enjoyed the privilege of providing healthcare to you over the years. I have learned many things from you as a patient that have only helped me become a better physician and a more empathic person overall, and I thank you for that.

It is with mixed emotions that I regret to inform you that as a result of multiple government regulations, the aspects of running a solo practice, and the financial aspects related to both, I will be closing my office on December 27, 2019.

This letter saddened me and motivated me to write this book. Here, I hope to clarify the root problem, identify the causes of the root problem, and, most important, offer solutions that will help reverse the forces that are robbing healthcare workers of the meaning, pride, joy, and purpose that come from caring for others. This book is a guide for healthcare leaders to navigate today's regulatory and financial pressures and to enable caregivers to rediscover the meaning and purpose that brought them into the healthcare profession in the first place.

Chapter 1 discusses in detail the factors that are diminishing the meaning and purpose of healthcare work and introduces a model of sustainable employee engagement. Chapter 2 articulates the central importance of personal and corporate values. Chapter 3 discusses how meaningful work is a function of vision and why meaning is critical to maximizing human performance. Chapter 4 shows how the alignment of organizational mission with individual motivation creates purpose in work that is the basis for sustainable employee engagement and long-term corporate achievement. Chapter 5 reviews the research on meaning and work. Chapter 6 begins to put together an employee engagement plan by focusing on creating a strong corporate culture. Chapter 7 explores how leaders set the vision that creates a transcendent purpose for all workers. Chapter 8 outlines several ideas for ongoing organizational and personal growth and development. Chapter 9 discusses what can go wrong when toxic executives behave badly and gives examples of what can happen when executives fail to understand the importance of the human factors necessary for long-term success. Chapter 10 brings together the key points of each chapter and recommends practical next steps.

This book was written while I was in isolation during the COVID-19 pandemic, as the healthcare industry was working under unprecedented conditions and facing an unknowable future. The public health crisis has highlighted the many unique and indispensable characteristics of healthcare professionals—not least their ability to risk their own personal safety for the benefit of those who are sick. The pandemic is perhaps the best illustration of the concepts discussed in this book: Meaning and purpose are the most powerful motivators of healthcare providers. Meaning and purpose are at the core of their beings. They are the manifestation of their souls.

—*Tom Atchison*

Acknowledgments

First, I want to thank all of you who have taken the time to read this book. I hope that the stories, interviews, concepts, and tools presented here are useful in solving your employee engagement leadership challenges.

My biggest thank-you goes to the outstanding leaders who made themselves available for interviews about their approach to employee engagement. Their input provided a wide spectrum of practical leadership suggestions about how to create a corporate culture that promotes sustainable employee engagement. These interviews took place during the COVID-19 pandemic in 2020 and 2021. These exceptionally busy healthcare leaders made time to share suggestions from their vast experience. Each person interviewed is a Servant Leader (Robert Greenleaf) and a Level 5 Leader (Jim Collins). These outstanding healthcare leaders include the following people:

- Carol Burrell, MHA, President and CEO, Northeast Georgia Health System, Gainesville, Georgia
- Karen Clements, RN, FACHE, Chief Nursing Officer, Dartmouth-Hitchcock Medical Center, Lebanon, New Hampshire
- Tina Freese Decker, MHA, MSIE, FACHE, President and CEO, Spectrum Health, Grand Rapids, Michigan
- Alan Kaplan, MD, FAAPL, FACHE, CEO, UW Health, Madison, Wisconsin

- Michael Mayo, DHA, FACHE, President, Baptist Health, Jacksonville, Florida
- Kurt Meyer, MA, Vice President, Human Resources/ Chief Human Resources Officer, Methodist Hospitals, Merrillville, Indiana
- Kim Miller, MBA, FACHE, President, Western Region Baptist Health, Fort Smith, Arkansas
- Scott Nygaard, MD, MBA, FCCP, Chief Operating and Medical Officer, Lee Health, Fort Meyers, Florida
- Samuel Odle, LFACHE, Senior Policy Advisor, Bose Public Affairs Group, Indianapolis, Indiana
- Brian Silverstein, MD, Consulting Director, The Chartis Group, Chicago, Illinois
- Rear Admiral Anne Swap, MPH, FACHE, Director, National Capital Medical Directorate, Defense Health Agency, Falls Church, Virginia
- Chris Van Gorder, EMT-B, MPA, FACHE, President and CEO, Scripps Health, San Diego, California

Thank you to Maria Gonzalez Zumbado for her research assistance. Special thanks go to my wonderful wife Lourdes for her patience, understanding, and tolerance while I took over (and trashed) our shared home office for five months. Finally, a thank-you goes to the Health Administration Press leadership and staff. A big thank-you goes to Deborah Ring, the editor who helped make this work more readable. This book would have not been written and published without the help and guidance of vice president Michael Cunningham, acquisitions editor Jennette McClain, and editorial production manager Andrew Baumann.

CHAPTER 1

A Model for Working in Today's Healthcare Environment

The only way to do great work is to love what you do.
—Steve Jobs

Pleasure in the job puts perfection in the work.
—Aristotle

People have enough to live by but nothing to live for;
they have the means but no meaning.
—Viktor Frankl

THE DYNAMICS OF TODAY'S HEALTHCARE INDUSTRY

The healthcare industry is changing in ways that are having deleterious effects on both workers and patients. Burnout among healthcare workers is a serious problem, as discussed in the preface to this book. According to the 2020 *Medscape National Burnout and Suicide Report*, 42 percent of physicians said they felt burned out. These data present a compelling case that healthcare workers, especially physicians, are dealing with serious, chronic mental and physical reactions to the increasing pressure to focus on the business of healthcare, at the expense of delivering care. As healthcare workers experience more and more burnout, patients are placed at greater risk of negative consequences while in hospital care.

According to a 2019 report published by the Leapfrog Group, more than 161,000 preventable deaths occur in hospitals annually. Another report from Johns Hopkins University, however, suggests this number is too low: An eight-year study determined that more than 250,000 deaths each year are attributable to medical errors. Dr. Martin Makary, a professor of surgery at the Johns Hopkins University School of Medicine, noted that "the medical coding system is designed to maximize billing for physician services, not to collect national health statistics, as it is currently being used." The study cautioned that most medical errors are not attributable to bad doctors. Rather, "most errors represent systemic problems, including poorly coordinated care, fragmented insurance networks, the absence or underuse of safety nets, and other protocols, in addition to unwarranted variation in physician practice patterns that lack accountability" (McMains 2016).

The conditions described in the Johns Hopkins study have existed for many years, and they have been exacerbated by the addition of the electronic medical record (EMR), which has changed the doctor–patient relationship. Dr. Michael Kirsch (2019) expressed the feelings of many, if not most, physicians on his blog: "These systems [EMRs] were not devised and implemented because physicians demanded them. To the contrary, they were designed to simplify and automate billing and coding. While this made their tasks considerably easier, it was at physicians' expense. Features that helped billers and insurance companies didn't help us take care of living and breathing human beings." This sentiment was echoed by Dr. Sam Slishman (2016), who wrote, "Electronic medical records offered an incredible opportunity to speed information transmission and improve care. But that promise has yet to be realized. I find they consistently pull me even farther away from my patients."

Merritt Hawkins, a physician search firm, analyzed the responses of nearly 9,000 physicians as part of its *2018 Survey of America's Physicians: Practice Patterns and Perspectives*. The survey demonstrated that the medical profession continues to struggle with burnout and low morale, identifying a number of alarming statistics:

- 80 percent of physicians said they are at full capacity or overextended.
- 55 percent described their morale as somewhat or very negative.
- 78 percent sometimes, often, or always experience feelings of burnout.
- 46 percent planned to change career paths.
- 49 percent would not recommend medicine as a career to their children.

The news was not entirely bleak, though. On the positive side, the Merritt Hawkins survey asked, "What two factors do you find *most* satisfying about medical practice?" Physicians' top answers were as follows:

- Patient/physician relationships, 78.7 percent
- Intellectual stimulation, 55.1 percent
- Social and community impact contributions, 21.0 percent
- Income/compensation, 18.9 percent
- Professional relationships with colleagues, 14.3 percent
- Professional stature of medicine, 9.8 percent

Similar responses could be elicited from most clinical and nonclinical staff working in healthcare systems. The universal erosion of morale in the healthcare industry can be explained by looking at the realities of living in a "VUCA" world.

HEALTHCARE IN A VUCA WORLD

In the late 1990s, the US Army used the abbreviation "VUCA" to describe the chaotic and unsettled environment that most army strategy and execution processes entailed. VUCA stands for *volatile, uncertain, complex*, and *ambiguous.* This book was written during the winter of 2020 and spring of 2021—in the middle of the COVID-19 pandemic and the beginning of our new post-COVID-19 reality. VUCA perfectly describes the current conditions affecting healthcare providers, patients and families, nonclinical healthcare professionals, and those in the general population who are concerned about their own health—the so-called worried well. The worldwide anxiety, fear, and uncertainty caused by the pandemic are unprecedented in our recent history. Working in healthcare before the COVID-19 pandemic was stressful. Now and for the foreseeable future, healthcare workers, especially direct care providers, will find it even more difficult.

In the spring of 2020, the *New England Journal of Medicine* published a thoughtful article titled "Lessons from CEOs: Health Care Leaders Nationwide Respond to the Covid-19 Crisis," in which CEOs from some of the largest healthcare delivery systems in the United States were interviewed. Dr. Tomislav Mihaljevic, CEO and president of the Cleveland Clinic, captured what the future may be like: "Traditionally, healthcare providers' core purpose has centered on caring for patients—as it always will be—but in contemporary health care our responsibilities have broadened. We care not just for patients, but for our fellow caregivers, our organization, and our communities." The way we approach each of these groups, Mihaljevic (2020) argued, will change in the future:

- Clinical care will be delivered increasingly through virtual platforms and at-home programs to minimize exposure of patients to the hospital environment.
- Caregivers and health care professionals will regain social recognition as noble and valuable members of

society, no longer treated like service workers or as a
commodity.

- Organizations that are arranged as integrated health
care delivery systems will emerge as the most efficient
platform for health care delivery, leading to a decline in
stand-alone hospitals and practices.
- Community care will be based on the integration of
social data and artificial intelligence, supplementing
episodic and occasional care.
- Finally, if the pandemic has taught us anything, it's the
need for increased funding to support vital research
and public health.

Mihaljevic's comments encapsulate the belief that the post-pandemic
healthcare delivery system will be irreversibility altered.

Now is a good time to embrace the lessons of VUCA dynamics:

- **Volatile.** Rapid and unpredictable change characterizes
the healthcare industry. The Affordable Care Act is
under pressure, driving uncertainty about payment for
services. Hospital systems are building urgent care centers,
emergency care centers, intermediate care centers, and
walk-in clinics, all in an attempt to lessen the use of
expensive emergency rooms and inpatient care. During the
pandemic, several innovative alternative delivery methods
were developed to meet the surge in COVID-19 cases. For
example, the use of telemedicine increased significantly
during the pandemic. Many hospitals struggled to care
for the increasing volume of very sick patients. To make
matters worse, by suspending elective surgeries, a prime
source of income was eliminated. It remains to be seen
which changes necessitated by the pandemic will become
permanent in healthcare. One treatment that seems
to be a part of our future is telemedicine. During this
volatile time, a few big questions emerge: How will the

US healthcare system be changed in terms of providing care, and how will the care be paid for? And, how many hospitals will close?

The COVID-19 pandemic placed extraordinary pressures on the healthcare delivery system, both in the United States and around the world. Physicians, other direct care providers, first responders, and system support personnel were all forced to work at more than 100 percent in dangerous conditions. Within this volatile environment, these people cared for those sick from the coronavirus, those sick and traumatized by events other than the virus, and an ever-growing population of the worried well. In anecdotal interviews with several direct care providers, comments clustered around some common themes, such as extreme fatigue, fear of catching the virus, fear of the unknown—will this virus ever be contained, and what will happen to my family if I get sick? A highly skilled nurse practitioner summed up the reality of care during the pandemic: "This is why I was drawn to medicine, yes. But I am worried about the spread of the virus and my personal health, and yes, I am very tired."

- **Uncertain.** Ask any physician, nurse, administrator, trustee, or other professional in any healthcare system: What will your role, responsibilities, and work expectations look like next year? Their answers will likely range from "I don't know" to "I don't know if I will even be working here." The uncertain world we live in reminds me of two famous quotes by Yogi Berra: "The future ain't what it used to be" and "It's tough to make predictions, especially about the future." Uncertainty brings up powerful emotions of fear and doubt. The medical issues associated with COVID-19, together with post-pandemic changes, may leave a trail of social and psychological concerns that have as great an effect on the future of healthcare delivery as the virus.

- **Complex.** Peter Drucker (2002, 74) described hospitals as the "most complex human organizations ever devised." Healthcare systems involve thousands of moving parts. For example, try to count the number of job titles in a typical tertiary hospital—the number could easily be over 100. Many, if not most, of these positions require specific degrees or credentials from a government body or professional society or association. The complexity of running a hospital or health system is made even more difficult by the ever-growing number of regulations and payment devices. On top of this "Gordian knot," we can add the many political actors who want to alter the US healthcare system or revise it completely.

- **Ambiguous.** Healthcare has many dimensions of ambiguity—organizational, professional, regulatory, financial, and societal. In many ways, the first three components of VUCA—volatile, uncertain, and complex—fuel the ambiguities that define today's healthcare delivery system.

While the healthcare industry experienced significant VUCA prior to the COVID-19 pandemic, the realities of this crisis and the post-pandemic world have taken the volatility, uncertainty, complexity, and ambiguity to new heights.

THE LEADER'S ROLE

The picture of healthcare delivery in the United States is muddled. One the one hand, the US healthcare system delivers thousands of lifesaving miracles each day. And yet the system is also fraught with fragmentation, frustration at all levels, role confusion, fear, uncertainty, and doubt. Given these realities, and understanding that financial and regulatory pressures will only increase in the future—is there an antidote?

The answer is yes. The key to sustainable success within a VUCA world is to create a corporate culture that allows all trustees, executives, physicians, nurses, clinicians, and professional support personnel to express meaning and find purpose in their work. Creating a culture based on sustainable employee engagement requires three pairs of critical elements: (1) values–alignment, (2) vision–meaning, and (3) mission–purpose. When leaders create a corporate culture based on these elements, the VUCA world will not disappear, but it will be secondary to high performance attributable to a highly engaged workforce.

THE MEANING AND PURPOSE MODEL

When VUCA factors dominate the work environment, they produce a workforce that is tired, stressed, uncertain, and fearful. The long-term corrosive effects of these negative feelings are immeasurable: low morale, high turnover, substandard performance, inter- and intragroup tension, and, too often, poor patient experiences. The regulatory and financial pressures that underpin today's VUCA environment are likely to continue and, quite possibly, increase. However, within this reality, there is a huge opportunity for healthcare leaders: to engage a workforce that is motivated by meaningful work within a purpose-focused organization. Meaning is fundamental to a worthwhile life. And purpose gives life transcendence.

Viktor Frankl's classic book *Man's Search for Meaning* is a good place to start to understand the importance of a meaningful life. Frankl (1959, 139) argued that "once an individual's search for a meaning is successful, it not only renders him happy but also gives him the capability to cope with suffering." This book will build on Frankl's premise as it applies to the healthcare work environment, today and in the future. As Frankl noted, "A human being is not one in pursuit of happiness but rather in search of a reason to become happy, last but not least, through actualizing the potential meaning inherent and dormant in a given situation" (138). How can healthcare leaders create a corporate culture in which all employees can actualize the "inherent and dormant meaning" in their "given situation"?

Let's begin to answer that question by reviewing some basic organizational dynamics. Exhibit 1.1 shows a grid with six interdependent cells that correspond with the main elements of all healthcare delivery systems. The grid lists the tangible and the intangible elements in healthcare delivery. The tangible elements can be measured using common statistical techniques, whereas the intangibles are the human factors that are more elusive to statistical measurement. Another way to think about the difference is to view the tangibles as the linear aspects of organizational dynamics and the intangibles as the nonlinear aspects. The tangible elements refer to the clinical and business outcomes in healthcare, such as morbidity and mortality

Exhibit 1.1 Tangible and Intangible Aspects of Healthcare Delivery Systems

	CORPORATE TANGIBLES	PERSONAL INTANGIBLES	CORPORATE INTANGIBLES
INPUTS	• Management • Cash • People • Policy/procedures • Strategy • Plant • Information systems • Communications	• Meaning • Caring • Giving	• Leadership • Mission • Values • Vision • Inspiration • Talent • Recognition • Motivation
OUTPUTS	• Profit • Market share • Customer satisfaction • Growth • Metrics • Quality	• Commitment • Joy • Pride • Purpose	• Culture • Followers • Commitment • Job satisfaction • Team spirit • Trust • Quality

rates on the clinical side and profit and market share on the business side. The intangibles are the human conditions of the workers, such as morale, team spirit, trust, engagement, and loyalty.

The exhibit also distinguishes between inputs and outputs. The best way to read this grid is to first identify the tangible and intangible outputs that you want to improve in your organization. Once the critical output elements have been determined, select the relevant input variables that you will need to measure and control to produce the desired output. For example, if you want more *profit* (a tangible output), you would measure the input factor of *strategy*. This same process can be used to affect the critical output of *purpose* by measuring and managing the critical input of *meaning*. The remainder of this book will show you how healthcare leaders can create a corporate culture in which the measurement and management of meaningful and purposeful work is a reality.

This grid shows the corporate tangible aspects of healthcare organizations (business and clinical), as well as the main corporate intangibles of healthcare organizations. These two columns are connected by the personal intangibles, which encompass the human factors that staff bring to an organization. It is in this center column that we find the characteristics that are most negatively affected by the VUCA world. The arrows show the direction of the elements. For example, the inputs drive the outputs, and the intangibles drive the tangibles.

Given that personal intangibles are the factors that are fueling burnout and low morale, what leadership priorities are required to reverse the deleterious dynamics of today's healthcare industry? Three pairs of critical elements are necessary to create a culture that ameliorates the destructive effects of our VUCA world. These pairs (in this sequence) are (1) values–alignment, (2) vision–meaning, and (3) mission–purpose. When leaders create a corporate culture based on these elements, the result is a high-performing organization driven by a loyal, committed, and engaged professional staff. The ultimate metric for leadership effectiveness is the degree to which everyone involved in healthcare believes that working in the

Exhibit 1.2 Key Elements of Corporate Culture

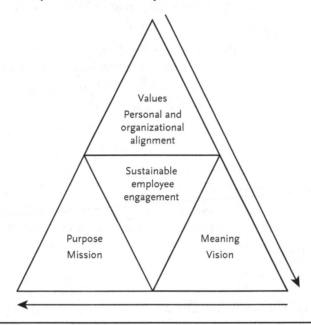

industry gives purpose to their lives. Exhibit 1.2 graphically depicts the factors that determine the degree of employee engagement and how they are interconnected.

These elements are the foundation and building blocks for the creation and ongoing strengthening of meaningful and purposeful work. These concepts are commonly used in discussions about organizational effectiveness. In the remainder of this book, I will show how these factors are not independent variables; rather, they are interdependent variables within organizational design. Each element alone can provide minimal opportunity for staff engagement. But when they are manifested in a structured, sequential, and developmental fashion, the resulting synergy is the basis for sustainable employee engagement. Too often in healthcare organizations, these words represent a vague statement written on a plaque that is displayed in the lobby or printed on the back of a name badge. And for some reason, there seems to be a strong attraction to creating an acronym, especially for a list of values. The role of today's healthcare leader is to convert these statements from jargon into descriptions of a powerful, positive corporate culture.

An important aspect of the model shown in exhibit 1.2 is that the elements are sequential. Everything begins with the alignment of an employee's personal values and the organization's core values. The alignment of individual and organizational values makes meaningful work possible. Once an employee finds the work meaningful, the power of the organization's mission and the motivation derived from its vision allow the employee to achieve a transcendent purpose. The formula is simple: Meaningful work plus corporate purpose equals sustainable engagement. While the model and formula are simple and easy to understand, the execution is more complex.

THE MODEL'S COMPONENTS

Personal Values

Values are the first and most critical component of sustainable employee engagement. Without alignment between personal and organizational values, there is no chance for meaningful work, much less engagement. A value can be defined as a belief that drives decision-making or behavior. Every individual has a unique set of values or beliefs that drive their decisions and behavioral choices. These subjective sets of values are the products of the individual's experiences throughout their lifetime. Social norms, family priorities, and religious beliefs are some of the most common sources of values. Some people posit the existence of innate, universal human values. In his article "Seven Innate Human Values: The Basis for Consistent Ethical Decision-Making," for example, Daniel Raphael (2020) presented the notion that all humans are born with seven values: life, equality, growth, quality of life, empathy, compassion, and love.

Scholars and philosophers will continue to debate whether we are born with a set of values or whether values are learned as we interact with society. For the purposes of this book, I make several assumptions about values: First, values are learned. Second, several types of values exist—for example, ethical/moral values, ideological/ political values, religious values, social values, and aesthetic values. Finally, our personal values are stable and resistant to change, but they do evolve over time. Notwithstanding their origin, personal values always underpin and control our choices. They guide our decisions by allowing for consistent individual choices regardless of the current environment. For example, an individual who values a healthy lifestyle will find time to exercise. This individual will be able to go to a buffet and select the most nutritious food items.

Our values influence and control our decisions and behavior at an unconscious level. The critical metric for analyzing values is behavior. Sometimes words and behavior may be in conflict. If someone says one thing but behaves in a contradictory fashion, then their words are lies. Kurt Vonnegut (2013) said it best: "We are who we pretend to be." We are our behaviors, not our words. So if a personal value is excellence, we can expect that individual to be scrupulous in their attention to detail. Conversely, if a person states that they believe in excellence but ignores details and produces sloppy work, we can determine that they do not truly value excellence. Behaviors are the outward representation of our values.

Corporate Values

All corporations are driven by a set of core corporate values. Typically, this is a short list of three to five values. Some corporations have more, maybe ten, values listed. However, it is hard to imagine that they are all equally relevant to daily decision-making. It seems reasonable to assume that most of the corporate decisions can be explained by a few values, such as financial viability, customer experience, market share growth, and employee engagement.

A corporation's core values determine its resource allocation, growth plans, and other critical business decisions.

An organization's core values drive all its important business decisions. If you observe a board of trustees meeting or an executive team meeting, you should expect to see the organization's core values embedded in the decisions made by those groups. As with personal values, if there is a difference between the values that the organization espouses publicly and the decisions made by trustees and executives, then the espoused values are false. Imagine that a board of trustees states that quality and a culture of safety are the core values of its healthcare delivery system. But this board also renews the credentials of a surgeon who has significantly higher morbidity and mortality rates than other physicians but generates considerable gross revenue. We can assume that the board's publicly espoused core values are just jargon. The real core corporate value is to maximize revenue regardless of clinical outcomes or patient safety.

Meaning

"Meaning in life" is the notion that all people are on a journey to find their reason for existence, and each person believes that their life has significance. The opposite of a life with meaning is a meaningless life.

The model depicted in exhibit 1.2 places values first and meaning second because meaning is found when our personal values match our life experiences. For an event or experience to have meaning, there must be a behavioral manifestation of values-based behavior. In this case, the environmental circumstances are favorable to the individual's values, and the resulting behavior is demonstrated consistently. For example, a clinician who is motivated by the value of quality will do everything possible to ensure the best care. In contrast, a clinician who is motivated by money will behave in a way that is driven by the question "Am I being paid for this work?"

There is an old story that supports the premise that values-based behavior is superior to just "getting it done." The story is about three bricklayers observed by the architect Christopher Wren in 1671 as they worked on the construction of St. Paul's Cathedral in London. One worker crouched down and moved very slowly. The second moved equally slowly. However, the third bricklayer stood tall and worked much faster than the others. Wren asked the men what they were doing. The first two responded that they were bricklayers, and they were laying bricks so that they could be paid for their work. The third bricklayer answered with enthusiasm, "I am a cathedral builder, and I'm building a great cathedral to the Almighty, my Lord and Master."

The lesson in this simple story is that there are levels of motivation, ranging from the mundane to the transcendent. In healthcare, the power of transcendent motivation is apparent when an employee's personal values are aligned with specific performance expectations. The secret to moving from values-based meaning to transcendent motivation—or purpose—is the organization's vision.

Mission/Vision

Mission and vision are combined in this employee engagement model because they are the "bookends" of the process of moving from meaningful work to finding purpose working in the organization. Remember, meaning results when personal values and corporate values are aligned. Purpose can be found in work when meaning exists within a greater context in which work moves from meaningful tasks and accomplishments to transcendence, as workers feel strongly connected to something greater than themselves. Individuals come to view meaningful work assignments as part of something much greater than their individual tasks. Purpose happens when individuals are connected to the organization's mission and know that they are contributing to something greater than themselves.

Imagine it is July 1969. You are employed by NASA to move materials as requested by the engineers. You drive a small tractor that carries materials and supplies needed to build the launch vehicle. In terms of the NASA hierarchy, you are at the low end of the pay grade. Now, it is July 20, 1969: The rocket is launched and lands successfully on the moon. Do you feel pride and joy on that day? Do you feel part of something greater? Do you celebrate with your family and friends because you were part of a historic day? The answer is probably yes to all of these questions.

While the moon landing may be an extreme example, major lifesaving successes occur every day in every hospital. Especially during the COVID-19 pandemic, many frontline workers and support staff found their work meaningful and reconnected with the purpose that prompted them to become healthcare providers.

The mission is the reason the organization exists, and the vision is an expression of where the organization wants to be in the future. Mission statements in healthcare delivery systems tend to be similar. Healthcare delivery exists to help the sick and encourage healthy communities. For example, Mayo Clinic's mission statement reads as follows: "Inspiring hope and promoting health through integrated practice, education, and research." The Mayo Clinic, quite possibly the most well-known healthcare delivery system in the United States, has a mission that focuses on the well-being of the whole person. Likewise, Grinnell Hospital, a small hospital in central Iowa, has a similar mission statement: "To improve the health of the people and communities we serve." Whether a healthcare delivery system is world renowned, like the Mayo Clinic, or a small rural hospital in Iowa, the reason it exists is to deliver care and promote health. Every organization exists for a reason—that is its mission.

The vision is a description of a future state that does not currently exist. It conveys a sense of what is possible, not what is probable. A vision statement contains three elements (it can have more, but it can't have less). The vision must be inspirational, directional, and measurable. Typically an organization's vision statement covers several years. The vision is the guiding principle for the organization's

Exhibit 1.3 Vision Guides Strategy, Tactics, and Performance

strategic planning, and the strategic plan drives the creation of departmental plans and individual performance objectives. Exhibit 1.3 shows the structure and dynamics of an organizational vision.

The vision is the bridge between values-based individual performance and the final component of the model—purpose. It is possible, and very common, for individuals to find meaning in their work but still be disconnected from the organization's mission. A staff member might say, "I love my job and my coworkers, but I have no idea what this organization stands for." Finding meaning in work when individual tasks help achieve the organization's vision is good, but it is not sufficient to sustain engagement. Sustainable engagement only comes from a strong connection to the transcendent purpose of the organization as described in the mission.

Purpose

Finding one's purpose in work is the highest level of personal achievement. People who find their work purposeful are highly motivated, passionate, excited to come to work, innovative, and great problem solvers. Purpose in life and work unleashes the best aspects of individuals. Ralph Waldo Emerson captured the essence of a purposeful life: "The purpose of life is not to be happy. It is to be useful, to be honorable, to be compassionate, to have it make some difference that you have lived and lived well."

Employees have purpose at work when they see how their efforts contribute to the achievement of the mission. Remember, meaningful work results when personal values are aligned with the core organizational values. It is possible to have meaningful work when connected to the vision, without being connected to the organization's greater purpose. It is the mission that takes workers from thinking about tasks and departmental objectives and helps them "transcend" their individual efforts to achieve something greater than their job—remember the cathedral worker who had a purpose greater than laying bricks!

A simple formula, which will be delineated in greater detail in the following chapters, explains the model: Personal values aligned with corporate values create the opportunity for meaningful work when tied to the vision, and a transcendent mission enables workers to be part of something greater than themselves—to have purpose. This sequence, when implemented properly, ensures sustainable engagement.

Profiles of Performance

Brian Silverstein: There Is No Healthcare System, Only a "Sick Care" System

Brian Silverstein, MD, is a consulting director at the Chartis Group, an independent healthcare advisory firm, and a member of the board of trustees of OSF St. Francis Health System in Peoria, Illinois. Brian is a thought leader on the past, present, and future of the healthcare industry. In an

(continued)

(continued from previous page)

interview, he explained, "There are so many forces at work in healthcare delivery. These forces have resulted in the current state of US healthcare, which does not work well for patients." Brian believes that it will probably get worse before it gets better because of the size and scope of the current financial and regulatory constraints. "Healthcare needs to innovate—it needs an 'Uber' experience, but such innovation is unlikely due to the way services are paid for." For example, Brian notes that insurance policies usually cover individuals for one year, but health, wellness, and management of chronic disease can take years to establish. That is why there is no "healthcare system," only a "sick care" system."

Brian has an interesting take on the COVID-19 pandemic and post-pandemic world. He believes that the pandemic may have exposed the things that people do *not* need from the healthcare system. And it has shown opportunities to use alternative methods to promote individual and community health—most notably, telemedicine. In addition, Brian concludes that the cultural reality of the US healthcare system is that individuals may live very unhealthy lifestyles but expect the local healthcare system to "fix" them, regardless of their personal choices. So far, there is no accountability or consequences for living an unhealthy lifestyle. Until the payment model for healthcare changes, we can expect little change in the behavior of those providing and receiving care in the US healthcare system.

Samuel Odle: Healthcare Is a Team Sport

Samuel Odle, LFACHE, is unquestionably one of the healthcare industry's most outstanding leaders. Sam is a senior

(continued)

(continued from previous page)

policy advisor for Bose Public Affairs Group. However, he began his healthcare leadership journey in 1981 as vice president of operations at Methodist Hospital in Indianapolis, Indiana. He retired in 2012 as CEO of both Methodist Hospital and Indiana University Hospital. His list of awards and honors is long and impressive. He is a fellow of the American College of Healthcare Executives and served on its Board of Governors from 2003 to 2006, including one year as chair.

Sam's multidecade perspective gives a clear picture of the changes that have taken place in the healthcare industry and how they have affected employee engagement. He recalled, "In the 1970s and early 1980s, there was a friendliness among healthcare leaders that went beyond collegiality. CEOs from hospitals in the same region wanted to collaborate." Then competition emerged in the payment environment. Sam suggested that this was a significant turning point in the US healthcare industry. "The payors wanted competition. The external environment kept changing. The factors driving change were external, not internal."

Mission and values are an important part of Sam's leadership philosophy. "The mission and values are my constant focus—my North Star. I have always used our core corporate values to drive decisions." He believes that it is important to be somewhat "evangelical" about the organization's mission and values. Sam's personal leadership style is based on the belief that healthcare's greatest assets are "the people who come to work every day to care for others." He noted, with much enthusiasm, that "healthcare is a team sport!" The biggest internal obstacle to employee engagement, he said, is the physician or staff member who is only concerned with "what's in it for me?"

SUMMARY

Today's healthcare delivery systems operate in a volatile, uncertain, complex, and ambiguous (VUCA) environment. The COVID-19 pandemic and our emerging post-pandemic reality have only exacerbated those qualities. The current pressures of the healthcare environment often result in an exhausted, frustrated, and sometimes angry clinical and executive workforce. The immediate, daily demands for quality clinical performance, as well as the demands for regulatory compliance and positive business returns, place constant pressures on everyone in the industry. There is, however, an antidote to the deleterious effects of the VUCA world: to refocus on the reason the healthcare delivery system exists, on the beliefs that drive decisions, and on the organization's goals for the future—that is, the mission, values, and vision. When these organizational elements are at the center of the daily work, workers will be able to fully engage because they can find meaning in their work and connect to the purpose of the organization.

QUESTIONS FOR ASSESSMENT AND DISCUSSION

Thinking about your own organization, respond to the following statements on a scale of 1 to 5, where 5 = strongly agree, 4 = agree, 3 = uncertain, 2 = disagree, and 1 = strongly disagree.

1. Our organization is ready for the VUCA world by adapting our services in ways that best serve our community.
2. Our organization balances the tangibles (the quantitative aspects) and the intangibles (the qualitative aspects) in all that we do.
3. Everyone in the organization understands and lives our mission, core values, and vision.

4. Clinicians and executives are partners in creating meaningful work and a purposeful organization.

5. The board of trustees' behavior and decisions are consistent with our mission, core values, and vision.

REFERENCES

Drucker, P. 2002. "They're Not Employees, They're People." *Harvard Business Review* 80 (2): 70–77, 128.

Frankl, V. 1959. *Man's Search for Meaning.* Boston: Beacon Press.

Kirsch, M. 2019. "How EMRs Changed the Doctor–Patient Relationship." Nimbus-T Global. Published August 13. https://nimbus-t.com/how-have-emrs-changed-the-doctor-patient-relationship/.

Leapfrog Group. 2019. "New Report Finds Risk of Death Nearly Doubles for Patients Using Hospitals Graded as 'D' or 'F.'" Published May 15. www.leapfroggroup.org/news-events/new-report-finds-risk-death-nearly-doubles-patients-using-hospitals-graded-"d"-or-"f".

McMains, V. 2016. "Johns Hopkins Study Suggests Medical Errors Are Third-Leading Cause of Death in U.S." John Hopkins University. Published May 3. https://hub.jhu.edu/2016/05/03/medical-errors-third-leading-cause-of-death/.

Medscape. 2020. *Medscape National Physician Burnout & Suicide Report 2020: The Generational Divide.* Published January 15. www.medscape.com/slideshow/2020-lifestyle-burnout-6012460?faf=1.

Merritt Hawkins. 2018. "2018 Survey of America's Physicians: Practice Patterns and Perspectives." Published September 18.

www.merritthawkins.com/news-and-insights/thought-leadership/survey/2018-survey-of-americas-physicians-practice-patterns-and-perspectives/.

Mihaljevic, T. 2020. "Lessons from CEOs: Healthcare Leaders Nationwide Respond to the Covid-19 Crisis." *NEJM Catalyst*. Published April 22. https://catalyst.nejm.org/doi/full/10.1056/CAT.20.0150.

Raphael, D. 2020. "Seven Innate Human Values: The Basis for Consistent Ethical Decision-Making." Accessed April 8, 2021. http://tmlife.org/seven-innate-human-values.html.

Slishman, S. 2016. "This Is What a Physician Wants in an EMR, Please Build It." KevinMD.com. Published April 24. www.kevinmd.com/blog/2016/04/this-is-what-a-physician-wants-in-an-emr-please-build-it.html.

Vonnegut, K. 2013. *We Are What We Pretend to Be: The First and Last Works*. New York: Vanguard Press.

CHAPTER 2

The Value of Values

*Your core values are deeply held beliefs that
authentically describe your soul.*
—John C. Maxwell

*When values, thoughts, feelings and actions are in alignment,
a person becomes focused and character is strengthened.*
—John C. Maxwell

*If you don't stick to your values when they're being tested,
they're not values, they're hobbies.*
—Jon Stewart

VALUES AND BEHAVIOR

Values rule! Our values drive our behavior. To know someone's values is to be able to predict with some accuracy how they will behave in a certain situation. If you watch a person's behavior in multiple situations over time, you can deduce—again, with some accuracy—their values. Our behaviors are the outward manifestations of our values. Exhibit 2.1 shows how values, emotions, feelings, and behaviors are related.

Values are the core around which our emotions, feelings, and behaviors are wrapped. Values are deep and subconscious, and they determine the degree to which we will adapt to our environment by

Exhibit 2.1 Values to Behaviors

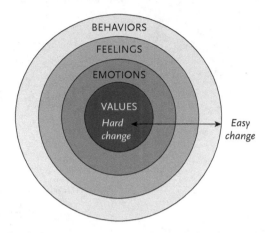

changing our behavior. The closer a behavioral expectation is to our core values, the easier it will be to accommodate that expectation—that is, to demonstrate a behavior. However, if a behavioral expectation runs counter to our core belief system, then it will be difficult, and maybe impossible, to change. Suppose, for example, that a nurse is asked to alter the treatment regime for the betterment of a patient. This request is consistent with the nurse's values, and most likely, she will make the requested change without any difficulty. However, if a nurse is asked to sell narcotics to children, the expected change is a grave contradiction of the nurse's values set, and she will not sell the narcotics. Quite simply, values determine our behavior.

Individuals have many values, but we assign more importance to some values than others. The relative weight of a personal value is controlled by the context. For example, the personal value of success might be an individual's number-one value at work, but the personal value of caring might be the most important value in raising a child. Think of personal values as an individual's context-controlled motivational hierarchy. The values that one considers most important are the primary drivers of all decisions in life, such as the choice of profession or career, religious preference, choice of mate, self-identity, and other major life determinants.

During the COVID-19 pandemic, we saw the remarkably positive response of physicians and other healthcare providers. It is easy to understand their extraordinary commitment to care, given the core values that brought them into the healthcare professions. These professionals, who risked their own health to care for those in need, did not complain about working long hours or needing more pay or other benefits. One of the lessons of the pandemic—and a fundamental message of this book—is that when our behavior is driven by our personal beliefs and core values (i.e., the intangibles that control our lives—see exhibit 1.1 in chapter 1), then our behavior *transcends* the most common tangibles in our lives—including time, money, and even fatigue.

In 2020, we saw daily posts on social media about the "healthcare heroes" of the pandemic. Each post captured the passion, commitment, and pride that these frontline professionals felt because they were helping to save lives. Their feelings of pride and ownership were the antidote to the stress, fear, and fatigue that healthcare workers felt increasingly every day. How could their feelings of pride, loyalty, commitment, and joy be so powerful, even during a difficult and dangerous crisis? The answer lies deep in the psyches of these "heroes." It lies in their values. When values manifest in a particular environment—such as a pandemic—the work becomes meaningful. When work has meaning and is seen as part of a greater good (the organization's mission and vision), then individuals have a deep sense of purpose.

Exhibit 2.2 illustrates the way in which values lead to purpose: Values create meaning in work. When the work is connected to the organization's mission and vision (see exhibit 1.2 in chapter 1), the individual finds purpose. That purpose, in turn, reinforces the individual's core values, and the cycle continues.

Where do our values come from? Behaviorists posit that at birth, each human is a *tabula rasa*—that is, a blank slate. According to this theory, humans have no innate beliefs at birth. Rather, all ideas, values, and beliefs are learned in the process of socialization in each culture. The development of personal values begins with the family. Parents, siblings, grandparents, and other family members are the

Exhibit 2.2 Values Create Meaning in Work

first people to imprint their values on a child. Then, of course, as the child grows older, friends, teachers, religious leaders, and others add to or reinforce the core values learned at home. Some theorists believe that an individual's core values are established during the first five or six years of life. These core values are resilient to significant change in the absence of trauma.

Humans possess many sets of learned values. We have beliefs about marriage, child-rearing, education, religion, and politics, just to name a few. However, as mentioned in chapter 1, *meaningful work* results from the alignment of one's personal values with an organization's core corporate values, as the individual sees their work as part of the achievement of the organization's vision. Finding *purpose* within an organization happens when the worker understands, accepts, and feels part of the mission.

PERSONAL VALUES

Personal values are strongly held beliefs that guide individuals' decisions and behavior. Individual values can be influenced by changing social values. The year 2020 provides a case in point, as a confluence of events prompted many Americans to examine, and in some cases reevaluate, their personal values. On May 25, 2020, George Floyd was killed by a police officer in Minneapolis, Minnesota. That incident—and others across the country—sparked a series of nationwide protests against the use of force by police. The Black Lives Matter movement, which focuses on combating systemic racism, was a powerful voice that summer. These national movements confronted many traditional personal and social values. These events took place against the backdrop of a tense presidential election and a pandemic that upended all our daily lives. The year brought a profound realignment of personal and social values that continues today. It seems clear, though, that the powerful reorientation of social values that we saw in 2020 will have an irreversible impact on our personal behaviors: how we work, from office to home; how students learn, from elementary school through college; how we view people who are different from us; how we use language, including pronouns; and how we make contact with other people. Will we ever shake hands or hug a friend again?

Our personal values are deep-seated. Therefore, significant societal disruptions do not necessarily change our personal values. Rather, we view those disruptions through the lens of our values. For example, a person who has a strong personal value of compassion will view the protests against police violence from a different perspective than a person who has a strong personal value of law and order. Neither of these individuals is wrong—they simply have different ways of looking at the same event. Too often, especially during times of dramatic social change, we say that others are wrong because they see and judge an event differently than we do. When it comes to personal values, some value-based perceptions may be more socially acceptable, but in fact, there are no right and wrong personal values, there are only different points of view. This fact is important to understand when personal and corporate values collide.

Empirical research on personal values is evolving. One of the earliest, best-known, and possibly most referenced is Abraham Maslow's (1954) hierarchy of needs (see exhibit 2.3).

Exhibit 2.3 Maslow's Hierarchy of Needs

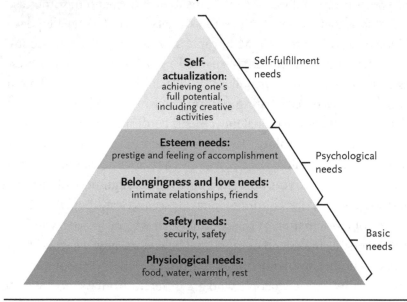

Source: Maslow (1954).

Maslow posited that human values are arranged in a hierarchy, with each level corresponding to an individual's current needs. His five categories of need are ranked from the most basic (physiological needs) to the most transcendent (self-actualization). For example, one cannot value love and belongingness (level three) unless one's physiological (level one) and safety needs (level two) have been met. Maslow's hierarchy of needs is useful for understanding some common behaviors. If a person is having difficulty meeting their financial needs, they may seek a job that pays the highest wage. This individual is not looking for a job that transcends their daily work and brings them pride and joy—they need money to pay the bills. They are locked in Maslow's first and second levels. There is some utility to Maslow's work. However, its simplicity may not be sufficient to explain the complexity of how values control our lives.

A more detailed, cross-cultural theory of personal values was created by Shalom H. Schwartz. His theory of basic human values accounts for the complexity of values regardless of background or culture. In a 2012 article, "An Overview of the Schwartz Theory of Basic Human Values," Schwartz detailed the ten basic human values that affect our daily life. Based on his research on values in 82 countries, he concluded, "Values are structured in similar ways across culturally diverse groups. This suggests that there is a universal organization of human motivations. Although the nature of values and their structure may be universal, individuals and groups differ substantially in the relative importance they attribute to the values" (Schwartz 2012, 3). Schwartz's ten universal values are security, conformity, tradition, self-direction, stimulation, hedonism, achievement, power, benevolence, and universalism (see exhibit 2.4).

Exhibit 2.4 Schwartz's Ten Universal Values

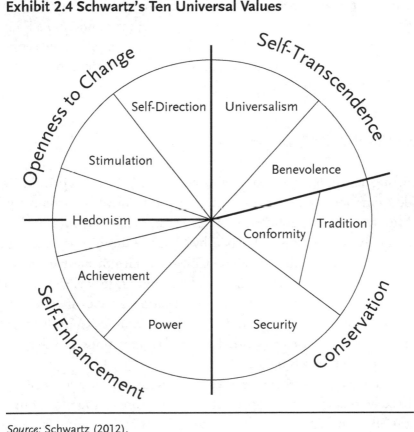

Source: Schwartz (2012).

Schwartz believed that all humans are motivated by the relative relationship among these ten values. He summarized his position on the nature of values with six key points (Schwartz 2012, 3–4):

1. Values are beliefs linked inextricably to affect.
2. Values refer to desirable goals that motivate action.
3. Values transcend specific actions and situations.
4. Values serve as standards or criteria.
5. Values are ordered by importance.
6. The relative importance of multiple values guides action.

In summary, there are some important facts about personal values: They are deeply held; they are initiated during our early socialization and enriched or modified throughout our lives; they are universal; they change and evolve slowly; they underpin all our decisions and behaviors; and each individual has a unique set of personal values that are more or less important depending on the environmental context.

ORGANIZATIONAL VALUES

All organizations have a core set of values and beliefs that drive their decisions about the current operation and future of the company. Most companies publicly display their values in many forums. For example, this book is published by Health Administration Press, which is a part of the American College of Healthcare Executives (ACHE). ACHE's core values can be found on its website and in many of its publications. Its core organizational values are *integrity*, *lifelong learning*, *leadership*, and *diversity and inclusion* (ACHE 2021). These values are used to guide its everyday operations as well as its strategic planning process.

An organization that uses its core values to guide decision-making is likely to have internal consistency and a strong corporate culture, as well as sustainable employee engagement and financial success.

However, an organization whose espoused corporate values are regarded as just "feel-good" jargon, and not drivers of behavior, is unlikely to sustain employee engagement or long-term success. For example, I can think of a healthcare organization that espoused employee satisfaction as a core corporate value and a strategic imperative. However, the organization's CEO approved a reduction in force of 60 professionals—many of whom were nurses—to be implemented before the end of the calendar year. His rationale was that the nurse-to-patient ratio was too high and needed to be adjusted. However, no data were presented to support that rationale. Later, it was revealed that the CEO had received a six-figure bonus as a result of the significant salary and benefits savings achieved by year's end. Needless to say, the obvious conflict between the organization's core value of employee satisfaction and the CEO's behavior caused irreversible damage to the organization.

There are a few simple ways to determine the degree of alignment between a healthcare organization's espoused values and the values that actually drive decisions and behaviors. For example, take a look at the healthcare organization's job posting for a direct care nursing position. Does the posting emphasize the organization's core corporate values, such as quality, compassion, and caring? Or does it emphasize the more tangible aspects of the job, such as good pay and benefits, signing bonuses, and free parking? When recruitment is focused on the monetary aspects of a position, it should be no surprise that employee engagement is a function of compensation. Organizationally, this means that it will be impossible for meaningful work and transcendent purpose to drive sustainable engagement. When an employee's connection to the organization is limited to pay and benefits, the motivation to perform at a high level is controlled by the individual's perception of whether "I get paid enough to do that." On the other hand, when personal values are aligned with the organization's core corporate values, the motivation is internal, and increasing performance expectations will be accommodated, because "That's the way we do it here." To be clear, there are no good or bad personal or corporate values. However, when the organization's professed core values are different from the values that actually motivate the staff, this misalignment contraindicates sustainable alignment.

Another simple way to determine the internal consistency between an organization's espoused values and the values that drive decisions and behaviors is to look at the board of trustees' agenda. Does the agenda begin with finance? Or does it begin with a discussion of important quality and safety data and end with financial consid- erations? Are physicians and nurses involved in board meetings? How many physicians and nurses are full voting members of the board? These metrics easily demonstrate the board's relative invest- ment in the clinical elements of its healthcare delivery responsibility compared with the business elements that support the delivery of healthcare services. Many for-profit hospitals and healthcare systems make it part of their mission and values to "maximize the return to the shareholders." In the case of for-profit organizations, the amount of discussion of revenue and expenses at the board level will (or should) be much greater than at a 501(c)(3), not-for-profit entity.

One quick way to determine the dominant values that drive decisions and behaviors is to ask the CEO, "How is everything at your facility?" If the CEO answers, "Really good, last month, we had a 2.57 percent positive return of revenue over expenses," then it is safe to assume that the business factors outweigh the clinical factors in decision-making. But if the CEO's answer is, "Really good, last month, our safety data was the highest this year, and this month looks even better," then it is clear that the organization's espoused values of quality and safety are driving its decisions and behaviors. Again, there are no right or wrong values—there is only internal consistency. To use a cliché, do the board and senior executives "walk the talk"?

An excellent example of core corporate values from a major, well- known healthcare delivery system comes from the Mayo Clinic. The Mayo Clinic (2021) lists the following core values on its website:

- **Respect**—Treat everyone in our diverse community, including patients, their families and colleagues, with dignity.

- **Integrity**—Adhere to the highest standards of professionalism, ethics and personal responsibility, worthy of the trust our patients place in us.
- **Compassion**—Provide the best care, treating patients and family members with sensitivity and empathy.
- **Healing**—Inspire hope and nurture well-being of the whole person, respecting physical, emotional and spiritual needs.
- **Teamwork**—Value the contributions of all, blending the skills of individual staff members in unsurpassed collaboration.
- **Innovation**—Infuse and energize the organization, enhancing the lives of those we serve, through the creative ideas and unique talents of each member.
- **Excellence**—Deliver the best outcomes and highest quality service through the dedicated effort of every team member.
- **Stewardship**—Sustain and invest in our mission and extended communities by wisely managing our human, natural and material resources.

The Mayo Clinic's core values are especially useful because each value is defined in terms of specific behaviors. This definition creates a universal understanding of what the Mayo Clinic means when it states that "respect" is a core value. Too many healthcare organizations leave their values undefined. When an organization lists words such as "quality," "caring," or "accountability," without any functional definition, then employees will create their own definitions. Quality is a good example. Ask any healthcare professional if their work is "quality" work. More than likely, you will hear, "Absolutely, my work is quality." But the degree to which each employee manifests the core value of "quality" in their work cannot be left to individual subjective assessment. It is critical for every healthcare organization to define its core values with a specificity that allows the demonstration of each value to be evaluated objectively. Just use Mayo Clinic as a "best case" model.

CORPORATE CULTURE: WHEN PERSONAL VALUES AND CORE CORPORATE VALUES CONVERGE

In chapter 6, I will go into more detail about the definition and dynamics of corporate culture. The relevance of corporate culture in this chapter is that values alignment determines the strength of any organization's corporate culture. The most important factor in the strength of any corporate culture is the degree to which the espoused public values are the true drivers of daily decisions and behaviors. A second, and equally important, factor is the alignment of employees' personal values with the organization's corporate values. High-performing healthcare organizations spend a great deal of energy and money to ensure a strong alignment of personal and organizational values. These organizations understand that their human capital capabilities and capacity to grow are the foundations of sustainable success.

The study of culture began in the discipline of anthropology. Scientists, most notably, Margaret Mead, wanted to know about cultural anthropology—the study of tribes and civilizations. The main question about culture is, What holds a people together? The answer may include things such as a common language, a shared history, a uniform currency, and, most important, a shared set of beliefs about right and wrong. An easy way to define a culture is that the behavior of the members of that culture is learned and not genetically determined. Our culturally appropriate behaviors are a function of our socialization, which begins at an early age and is reinforced through multiple interactions with other members of the culture.

Another way to describe cultural accommodation is that it is what we do when no one is looking. In other words, our culturally driven behaviors are "subcortical" or "reflexive." These imbedded, hardwired, culturally learned behaviors are very resistant to change.

The reason is that culturally learned behaviors are the dominant values of that culture. Those who are raised in a capitalist culture—for example, the United States—may behave in ways that produce the most money for themselves. However, those who are raised in a socialist country—for example, Costa Rica—may behave in ways that support the greater good for the group. Remember, as mentioned earlier, there are no good or bad values, or values-based behaviors. Rather, behaviors are either culturally aligned or misaligned.

HEALTHCARE CULTURE

All corporate cultures possess the same fundamental traits. Strong corporate cultures are anchored by the organization's mission (the reason the company exists), vision (the company's desired future destination), and, most important, core corporate values (the company's decision rules). Likewise, healthcare delivery systems with strong corporate cultures are also grounded by the critical factors of mission, vision, and values. However, there are some differences between healthcare and other industries, such as the way services are paid for and the wide variability in outcomes. The most important difference is that no other industry has physicians.

As a society, we have a cultural expectation that healthcare services should be readily available on demand, very high in quality, and free or very inexpensive. In the United States, if you want to buy a car, you negotiate the price and pay the agreed-upon amount. Imagine if 80 percent of the price of a car were paid for by a third party. Customers would view the total price very differently. This is one of the main cultural differences in the US healthcare industry. It is rare for a patient to ask the price of a desired healthcare consultation or procedure. Patients assume that the cost they pay will be a small fraction of the total cost.

Another cultural reality of the US healthcare system is the assumption that services should be readily available and of high quality. In other countries that control the total national budget for healthcare, patients must queue for services. But the idea of waiting months to see a specialist is unacceptable to patients in the United States. And, if a patient in the United States receives an unacceptable outcome, legal remedies are available. It is estimated that legal liability claims accounted for 2.4 percent of the $3.6 trillion total annual healthcare expenses in 2020.

The factor that most distinguishes the culture of the US healthcare industry is the role of physicians. A healthcare system cannot exist without physicians. But in today's healthcare delivery, we are seeing a significant increase in the use of nurse practitioners (NPs) and physician assistants (PAs) to perform tasks that once were done exclusively by physicians. There are two main reasons for this growth: the ever-growing physician shortage, especially in rural areas, and the cost savings of using NPs and PAs.

The dominant values held by physicians are different from the values held by NPs, PAs, other clinicians, and healthcare executives. Exhibit 2.5 depicts the values-based differences between

---

Exhibit 2.5 Five Values-Based Differences Between Physicians and Executives

Organizational Dynamics
Physicians---Executives

Decision Process
Control ---------------------- Influence

Perception of Time
Now -------------------- Long Range

Sense of Self
Protection of Individual Prerogative---Part of a Team

Locus of Control
Practice Needs------------Corporate Strategy

First Loyalty
To the Patient ----------------- To the Corporation

---

physician and executive behavior in five key domains. These values-based dynamics are a consequence of the socialization process that physicians undergo during medical school, which differs significantly from the socialization process of an administrator pursuing a master of health administration (MHA) or master of business administration (MBA) degree.

The first difference between physicians and executives is the way they make decisions. Physicians have a lot of control—they write "orders"—whereas executives have little control but a lot of influence. Executives need to influence the board of trustees, the staff, and the community. The second difference between physicians and executives has to do with their perception of time. Physicians live in a "stat" world. They need to be exceptionally efficient in their use of time. In a physician's world, now means now! In contrast, the typical time frame for an executive's planning may cover one, three, or five years. In fact, some master building plans can cover ten years or more.

These value differences between physicians and executives can cause serious problems. The most devastating interaction between physicians and executives in regard to their different perceptions of the first two dynamics—decision process and perception of time—is the "slow no." The slow no happens when an executive does not want to give a physician bad news, so instead of being direct and saying clearly that the physician's request will not be granted, the executive says something like, "I'll review your request and discuss it with my team, it should be a few weeks before we will have an answer." The executive may hope that the physician will forget about the request, thereby avoiding the need to deny it. Unfortunately, most physicians are tenacious when it comes to something they want or need for their practice. So, after a couple of weeks, the physician will ask for a decision, and the executive will make up a reason for another delay. This repeated process of a physician making a request and the executive delaying action on the request is the "slow no," and it is extremely toxic to physician engagement.

The third fundamental difference between physicians and executives is the most important. The most basic value of all physicians is the *absolute protection of the individual prerogative*. There is a saying that if you have worked with one physician, you have worked with one physician. It is impossible to generalize the behaviors of even a small group of physicians. The reason for this individualism has a lot to do with the socialization of physicians during medical school and residency programs, where the road to success is very competitive. There are few, if any, opportunities for team performance in medical school. In contrast, in many MHA and MBA programs, students are often graded on the basis of team performance. To illustrate this dynamic, consider the difference between golf and volleyball. The performance expectation of someone playing on a golf team, such as the Ryder Cup, is individual excellence on a par with other three excellent team members. This expectation is radically different from that of a volleyball team, where the coordinated performance of six players determines the outcome.

The fourth difference between physicians and executives is the way they view information, especially regarding changes in processes and procedures. Physicians listen through a filter: "How is this change going to affect my practice?" However, healthcare executives typically make decisions based on the best data available for the greater benefit of the entre healthcare system. Difficulties can arise when a physician group feels that a corporate decision is counterproductive to their practice. For example, a surgical group with several older members may feel threatened when the healthcare system says that it needs to recruit younger surgeons. There is a unique communication phenomenon that happens when executives believe they are making decisions based on the best long-term interests of the organization, but a specific physician group sees it as an immediate threat. This communication principle is, "In the absence of complete information, the information void is always filled with negativity." The antidote to that negativity is for the executive to engage any physician groups that might feel threatened by a systemwide decision early in the decision-making process. The group may not always agree in the end, but physicians will better understand the decision.

The final values-based difference between physicians and executives is focus: The executive must focus on what is best for the corporation, while the physician must focus on what is best for their patient. The difficulty here often concerns the cost of treating a patient. A long hospital stay may seem like the best practice for a physician, while the executive sees a hospital stay that is longer than what the patient's insurance will pay for as an unnecessary business expense. Most healthcare systems have drafted protocols for length of stay and the use of procedures. The most successful protocols are those created by physicians and executives working in partnership.

Profiles of Performance

Carol Burrell: Organizational Success Is Anchored by Our Core Values

Many healthcare systems have strong, vibrant corporate cultures. A common characteristic of such systems is that they are led by a president or CEO who builds a culture based on the core corporate values. An example is Northeast Georgia Health System (NGHS) in Gainesville, Georgia. Carol Burrell is the president and CEO of NGHS. She took the position in 2010, after having served as chief operating officer for 11 years. When Carol took the helm at NGHS, the system had one hospital with approximately 3,000 full-time employees. Today, NGHS encompasses four hospitals with approximately 8,000 full-time employees. Carol has led a great deal of change. During the pandemic, she dealt with the significant challenges posed by COVID-19, and yet she continues

(continued)

(continued from previous page)

to pursue a vision of growth that promotes the NGHS mission of fostering a healthier community.

All of these decisions are anchored by NGHS's four core values. The development of these four values was the result of a thorough process that engaged approximately 150 staff members, physicians, and trustees. The process involved small focus groups analyzing pictures that spoke to the values being portrayed at NGHS. From this detailed process, four values were determined to capture the essence of the system:

> NGHS prides itself on four core values, all of which help us achieve our mission of improving the health of our community in all we do. These values shape the daily interactions between our physicians, staff, volunteers, board members, patients and their loved ones.
>
> Respectful compassion—I impact life's most sacred moments.
> Responsible stewardship—What I do today ensures tomorrow.
> Deep interdependence—I can't do my job without you.
> Passion for excellence—I bring my best every day.

NGHS's ongoing success with expansive growth of clinical services, dealing with a serious pandemic, and constantly moving toward a healthier community is built on the strong foundation of these four core values.

Note to the reader: Please go to NGHS's website (www.nghs.com/core-values/) to see how these four values are presented. Notice that for each of the values, there is a tagline. For example, the value "respectful compassion" is followed by a short statement about what this value means to the

(continued)

(continued from previous page)

individual: "I impact life's most sacred moments." Alongside each value on the website is a short video of what that value means to the staff member. The combination of the value, the tagline, and the video is very powerful.

SUMMARY

The value of values cannot be overstated in terms of creating a corporate culture that promotes sustainable engagement. A person's values must be in line with the core corporate values of the organization. Even the slightest conflict between personal and corporate values will limit staff engagement. Personal values are unique to the individual, and to a great degree, they are determined by our early socialization. Our parents, extended family, religious community, schools, and friends all influence our core values and beliefs. Our values drive our decisions and our behaviors. When our personal values are matched with an organization's core values, long-term, sustainable engagement is possible. However, when personal values and core corporate values are in conflict, engagement will never be stronger than a paycheck.

QUESTIONS FOR ASSESSMENT AND DISCUSSION

Thinking about your own organization, respond to the following statements on a scale of 1 to 5, where 5 = strongly agree, 4 = agree, 3 = uncertain, 2 = disagree, and 1 = strongly disagree.

1. Our organization has a clear, well-known set of core values.
2. Everyone knows the expected behaviors for each of the organization's core values.

3. Our core values are used to recruit, interview, hire, and orient new employees.

4. Everyone in the organization can describe "who we are" and "what we stand for."

5. Values-based behavioral clashes are dealt with swiftly.

REFERENCES

American College of Healthcare Executives (ACHE). 2021. "Strategy." Accessed May 12. www.ache.org/about-ache/strategy.

Maslow, A. 1954. *Motivation and Personality*. New York: Harper Brothers.

Mayo Clinic. 2021. "Mayo Clinic Mission and Values." Accessed May 12. www.mayoclinic.org/about-mayo-clinic/mission-values.

Schwartz, S. H. 2012. "An Overview of the Schwartz Theory of Basic Human Values." *Online Readings in Psychology and Culture*. Published December. https://doi.org/10.9707/2307-0919.1116.

CHAPTER 3

The Meaning of Meaning

For in the end, it is impossible to have a great life unless it is a meaningful life. And it is very difficult to have a meaningful life without meaningful work.
—Jim Collins

If you wanted to crush and destroy a man entirely, to mete out to him the most terrible punishment . . . all one would have to do would be to make him do work that was completely devoid of usefulness and meaning.
—Fyodor Dostoyevsky

Work gives you meaning and purpose, and life is empty without it.
—Stephen Hawking

WHY MEANING IS IMPORTANT IN WORK

High-performance healthcare delivery systems effectively balance the tangibles and the intangibles. But in today's environment, there is one critical factor that determines success—*meaning*. Exhibit 3.1 revisits the organizational dynamics of healthcare delivery systems introduced in chapter 1. The exhibit shows the interrelationships between and among corporate tangibles, corporate intangibles, and the "connective tissue" of personal intangibles.

Exhibit 3.1 Tangible and Intangible Aspects of Healthcare Delivery Systems

	CORPORATE TANGIBLES	PERSONAL INTANGIBLES	CORPORATE INTANGIBLES
INPUTS	• Management • Cash • People • Policy/procedures • Strategy • Plant • Information systems • Communications	• Meaning • Caring • Giving	• Leadership • Mission • Values • Vision • Inspiration • Talent • Recognition • Motivation
OUTPUTS	• Profit • Market share • Customer satisfaction • Growth • Metrics • Quality	• Commitment • Joy • Pride • Purpose	• Culture • Followers • Commitment • Job satisfaction • Team spirit • Trust • Quality

To understand this grid and its application to creating a sustainable, high-performing healthcare delivery system, some definitions are necessary. The tangible elements are easy to measure using common quantitative statistical techniques, whereas the intangibles are the human factors that are more difficult to capture. To measure intangibles, techniques such as Likert surveys and structured interviews are typically used. However, these kinds of qualitative, nonlinear metrics do not have the same precision as quantitative, linear metrics. Consequently, intangibles are considered the "soft stuff" of organizations. And yet, the intangibles are the things that determine the degree of meaningful work and, ultimately, sustainable employee engagement within the organization. Based on the current state of healthcare delivery, we might posit that the intangible, qualitative elements are hard to measure and manage, and the tangible, quantitative elements are easy to measure and manage. In today's healthcare, the "soft stuff" is hard, and the "hard stuff" is easy.

Exhibit 3.1 also shows the inputs and outputs of the primary corporate tangibles, corporate intangibles, and personal intangibles. The arrows indicate that the intangibles drive tangible performance, such as profit, market share, and customer satisfaction. However, this premise is breaking down—in fact, the reverse is now happening. That is, the tangible factors of revenue, profit, and performance expectations are driving the intangibles. In today's healthcare environment, the tangibles are overwhelming the intangibles—both the corporate intangibles, such as culture and trust, as well as the personal intangibles, most importantly, meaningful work.

In a report for McKinsey & Company, Dan Cable and Freek Vermeulen (2018) note that "By now, it is well understood that people who believe their job has meaning and a broader purpose are likely to work harder, take on challenging or unpopular tasks and collaborate effectively. Research repeatedly shows that people deliver their best effort when they feel part of something larger than the pursuit of a paycheck." Likewise, Teresa Amabile and Steven Kramer (2012) report on a multiyear study that "found that of all the events that can deeply engage people in their jobs, the single most important is making progress in meaningful work."

Meaningful work occurs when the conditions within the organization are such that leaders are constantly connecting employees' daily goals and tasks to an inspiring vision or an important strategic goal. Compare this description of meaningful work with the seemly ever-present demands to "hit the numbers," "complete your charts," "do more with less," "cut costs," and other soul-sucking phrases that underpin subpar performance.

The meaning of meaning in work is that those involved in the daily operations of the organization—at all levels—feel a sense of control over the decisions that affect their work, have high-quality interactions with others, have a clear sense of direction, and understand their role in the organization's progress in the desired direction. There is a sense of ownership—psychic equity—as well as a confidence that "I have a future here!"

Here is a quick test to determine whether your employees have found meaningful work. Ask a randomly selected group of physicians and staff to answer yes or no to the following statements:

1. I feel valued.
2. I am clear about my daily roles and responsibilities.
3. I have a strong social network in this organization.
4. I have a future with this organization.

In high-performing organizations, employees consistently answer yes to all of these questions. The questions are diagnostic, as each comes with prescriptions for change. If an employee answers no to question 1, that individual needs to be rewarded and recognized more (see chapter 7 for motivation tools). If an employee answers no to question 2, clearer and more detailed role expectations need to be put in place (see chapter 8 for communication tools). If question 3 elicits a no answer, team-building exercises can be helpful (see chapter 10 on effective team building). And, if the answer to question 4 is no, the leadership must clearly explain the organization's long-term vision and detail how each employee is critical to the achievement of this vision.

Employees who find meaning in their work are those whose personal values are aligned with the corporate values and are able to connect their work to the company's vision and strategic plan. The multitude of daily tasks that an employee performs makes the work meaningful because each task demonstrates that employee's commitment to positive performance. Compare the performance of an employee who is motivated to work because a task has meaning with an employee who completes a task because otherwise they won't be paid. Money is a powerful motivator, but it is a severely limited tool when trying to lead an organization to a high level of excellence. (A detailed discussion of money as a motivator is presented in chapter 5.)

THOUGHTS FROM RESEARCH

Human beings are constantly searching for meaning in their lives. Erich Fromm, a noted social psychologist and psychoanalyst, has written extensively on the subject of humans' deep-seated need to find meaning in life and a purpose to live for. Fromm's work echoes that of Viktor Frankl, discussed in chapter 1. Fromm (2019) believes that "the whole life of the individual is nothing but the process of giving birth to himself." He continues, "There is no meaning to life except the meaning man gives his life by the unfolding of powers." And, "Man does not suffer so much from poverty today as he suffers from the fact that he has become a cog in a large machine, an automaton, that his life has become empty and lost its meaning."

In their McKinsey & Company report, Cable and Vermeulen state what should be obvious: "People who find meaning at work are happier, more productive and *more engaged*." In another McKinsey article written by Rodgers Palmer and Bill Schaninger (2018), the authors extend the notion of meaningful work as "the link between meaning and organizational health." They note that meaningful work occurs when "leaders connect daily work to a grander goal." Palmer and Schaninger posit that "organizational health is correlated with financial performance," and they believe that the health of an organization is a function of the degree to which employees find meaning in their work. In other words, meaningful work creates a healthy organization, and a healthy organization has positive financial performance.

Palmer and Schaninger argue that three elements must be in place for employees to view their work as meaningful. The first and most important is "'direction'—the ability to give employees a clear sense of where the organization is headed." The second critical determinant of meaningful work in a healthy organization is "the quality of employee interactions, measured through the strength of the 'work environment' . . . 'open and trusting' workplace behavior is a critical contributor to a strong work environment." The third critical determinant of meaningful work is "giving people a sense of ownership and control," which "contributes to a greater sense of accountability, to a better work environment, and to stronger execution skills."

Mihaly Csikszentmihalyi has researched and written extensively on a concept of optimal human behavior called "flow." In general, flow is a state of mind in which we unleash our full potential in the activities that are part of our daily lives. According to flow theory, when individuals are fully engaged in their jobs, time is suspended, efficiency and quality are improved, productivity is increased, and innovations are produced. Flow is the connection of values, meaning, and purpose. Csikszentmihalyi (1997, 62) believes that "it is not the external conditions that determine how work will contribute to the excellence of one's life. It is how one works, and the experiences one is able to derive from confronting its challenges."

The research summarized here provides some excellent philosophical and practical insights and tools for healthcare leaders who wish to increase employee engagement by fostering meaningful work. Frankl and Fromm present a strong case for a fundamental, innate, cross-cultural drive among all human beings to find meaning in their lives. This philosophical principle is in line with what was outlined in chapter 1. Values are critical for recruiting, interviewing, hiring, and onboarding physicians and staff. When physicians and staff are confident that the board of trustees and executive leadership are using an agreed-upon set of core values to drive their decisions, then, as Frankl, Fromm, and Csikszentmihalyi suggest, work is an arena in which to find meaning. Palmer and Schaninger's definition of "meaningful work" directs leaders to a specific process for increasing meaning in work—a sense of direction.

The model presented in this book, introduced in chapter 1, contains three domains that must be in place for sustainable employee engagement. First, personal values and core corporate values must be aligned; second, employees must find meaning in their work; and third, employees must find a greater purpose (see exhibit 1.2 in chapter 1). The model shows the sequence of a healthcare leader's process of moving employees from values to purpose.

LEADERSHIP APPLICATION

Once personal values and corporate values are aligned, the opportunity for meaningful work can emerge. Remember, without aligned values, there is little or no possibility for meaningful work to occur. An individual moves from working on a task to working for meaning when the task is connected to the organization's vision. The vision is important for several reasons. The most important reason is that employees can see how their specific work assignments contribute to the long-term success of the healthcare delivery system.

Visions have several characteristics: They are forward looking. They describe a destination—a future state that is better than the current situation. All visions have three key characteristics: They are inspirational, directional, and measurable. (Exhibit 1.3 in chapter 1 shows the relationship between and among the elements of a vision statement and individual performance.)

Leaders create an inspirational, directional, and measurable vision that serves as the transcendent purpose of all organizational efforts. Visions typically span several years. In healthcare a 3-, 5-, or even 10-year vision is common. The corporate vision statement is best constructed through a process that includes the trustees and senior executives. Some organizations also include staff and community members in the vision development process. However, this is not an effective way to develop a vision. A vision statement must be the product of governance and senior executives—*the head must lead the body*. After the initial vision statement is written, it is useful to share it with staff and community members to collect ideas for the next phase of engaging employees in meaningful work: the construction of a strategic plan.

While the creation of a vision is the responsibility of the trustees and senior leadership, the development of a strategic plan should include staff, community members, and patients and their families. Strategy development must be guided by the question, Do these strategic imperatives move us closer to the achievement of our vision? If the answer is yes, then the strategic imperative is included. Too often, strategic planning focuses on today's "hot issue" without regard for whether it moves the organization toward achieving its vision. Vision statements set the "guardrails" for deciding what the strategic plan will include.

First, the inspirational, directional, and measurable vision is created by senior leaders; next, the strategic plan is developed with maximum input from multiple stakeholders; then, tactical plans can be formed by department heads. Tactical plans establish the departmental goals. They set goals and metrics for a period of time, typically three months. These departmental tactical plans are the source of individual performance objectives and metrics for each employee. When visioning and strategic and tactical planning are done this way, individual employees understand how their daily tasks contribute to the long-term success of the organization. This process makes it possible for employees to find meaning in their work and to be fully engaged.

The process of visioning drives many of the decisions we make in our personal lives, even though we may not call it such. Some common examples of how we use visioning in our personal lives are planning a vacation, building a house, and a funding a retirement plan.

The first thing we do when planning a vacation is to select a destination that is highly desirable—that is, inspirational and directional—and we can measure when we arrive. The identification of a destination, or a vacation "vision," drives the strategic, tactical, and individual performance goals to get to the destination. Tactical planning might include saving for the trip, asking for time off, buying beachwear, buying plane tickets, reserving a hotel, and so on.

Likewise, we use the visioning process when building a house. The first step is to design the plans. What will the house look like and contain when it is completed? A blueprint is a vision statement that drives the scheduling and sequencing of all the contractors.

Finally, a retirement plan is a vision in action. Typical retirement planning begins with a question: How much money do I need to retire comfortability? In other words, retirement planning starts with an inspirational, directional, and very measurable vision. Once the "endgame" has been identified, then the strategic, tactical, and individual performance requirements of systematic deposits plus the benefit of compound interest will help you achieve your retirement vision. These simple examples illustrate the power of an organizational vision that connects employees to meaningful work.

One caveat needs to be addressed when speaking about vison statements. There is an important difference between a vision and a slogan. A vision, by definition, is inspirational, directional, and measurable. A vision describes a future that is better than today. A slogan, on the other hand, is inspirational but omnidirectional and unmeasurable. The best example of a slogan is Nike's: "Just Do It." This slogan is inspirational but does not give direction, nor is there anything concrete that can be measured.

All high-performing organizations, in healthcare and in other industries, have a vision that connects the employees' tasks to success in a meaningful way. Here are some classic examples of corporate vision statements:

- **Tesla:** "To create the most compelling car company of the 21st century by driving the world's transition to electric cars."

- **Amazon:** "To be the Earth's most customer-centric company, where customers can find and discover anything they might want to buy online."

- **Patagonia:** "To save the wild and beautiful places, and to help reserve the steep decline in the overall environmental health of our planet."
- **Google:** "To provide access to the world's information in one click."
- **Toyota:** "To be the most successful and respected car company in America."
- **Southwest:** "To be the world's most loved, most flown, and most profitable airline."

All of these corporate vision statements contain the basic elements: They are inspirational, directional, and measurable. It is easy to see how these vision statements could be the basis for strategic and tactical planning. And, most important, these vision statements easily provide meaning to employees' daily tasks.

The most successful healthcare systems have powerful vision statements. Here are a few examples:

- **Mayo Clinic:** "Mayo Clinic will provide an unparalleled experience as the most trusted partner for health care."
- **Cleveland Clinic:** "To be the best place for care anywhere and the best place to work in healthcare."
- **Scripps Health:** "To be the leading health care delivery system in the greater San Diego community, as evidenced by the highest clinical quality, patient safety, and patient, physician, and employee satisfaction."
- **Ascension Health:** "We envision a strong, vibrant Catholic health ministry in the United States which will lead to the transformation of healthcare."
- **Baptist Health:** "To lead in clinical excellence, compassionate care, and growth to meet the needs of our patients."
- **Cardinal Health:** "To be the premier global healthcare company as recognized by current and potential customers, employees, and shareholders."

THE BRIDGE FROM VISION TO
MEANINGFUL WORK: TRUST

Vision statements are useful for transforming employees' tasks from mundane to meaningful—but only when employees can see how their efforts fit into the organization's future. The conversion of a written vision statement into a motivational tool requires that employees trust the senior leadership, especially the CEO. The two requirements for sustainable employee engagement are aligned values (discussed in chapter 2) and trust among employees and between employees and the CEO.

Trust is a complex and elusive dynamic. But without trust, it is impossible to maximize organizational potential through sustainable employee engagement. In his book *The Speed of Trust*, Stephen Covey (2006, 69) states that "trust is the one thing that changes everything." Trust has several unique qualities:

1. Trust is the perception of honesty, openness, and reliability.
2. Trust increases as a function of active listening.
3. Trust takes a long time to develop.
4. Trust can be weakened or broken easily.
5. Trust is the glue and lubricant for sustainable success.
6. Trust is different from likeability—there is no relationship between being liked and being trusted.

Let's take a more in-depth look at these six qualities of trust.

1. **Trust is the perception of honesty, openness, and reliability.** Healthcare leaders earn trust when employees believe that they are telling the truth, telling them everything that is important, and conveying a consistent message. Because the trust bond between employees and leadership is perceptual, the strength of the bond is

symbolic. That is, the leader symbolizes either trust or mistrust. This fact is especially important when there is a change in leadership. If the new CEO replaces someone who was highly trusted, the new CEO will symbolize positive trust and, most likely, will be believed. However, if the new CEO replaces someone who was not trusted, the new CEO will be saddled with feelings of mistrust. The practical application of viewing trust as perception is that leaders need to understand their symbolic trust value whenever they change positions.

2. **Trust increases as a function of active listening.** Communication is considered the main avenue for building trust. Too often, however, communication is limited to talking. When building trust with employees, listening is more important than talking. Effective listening is the most powerful tool leaders can use to increase the trust bond with employees. The ability to listen and understand is key to building trust. Three types of listening are common in organizations: selective and judgmental listening; active listening; and reflective listening. Selective and judgmental listening is far too common and not only does not build trust, it creates mistrust. Selective and judgmental listening happens when the leader hears a part of a statement and then interrupts with a comment or conclusion. For example, an employee talks to a supervisor about the increased effort required to deal with the COVID-19 pandemic and the supervisor interrupts the employee to say, "That's just the way it is now, we are all working harder." In this case, the employee may have been requesting a little empathy and was met with a rather harsh directive. Thus, the employee learns that going to the supervisor is a waste of time. The same interaction would have a very different result if the supervisor used active listening techniques.

Active listening is characterized by the use of questions. Let's again use the example of an employee talking to a supervisor about the extra stress of providing care during a pandemic. In the previous example, the supervisor interrupted the employee and essentially said, "Life is tough, get back to work." This judgmental approach completely eliminates the possibility of trust between the employee and the supervisor. When the supervisor uses active listening, the response is a series of questions. The supervisor might ask, "What do you find most taxing?" or "How are you coping with this increased stress?" After a series of clarifying questions, the active listening process always ends with the same question: "How can I help you solve this problem?" It is important to the trust-building process that the employee is heard and knows that the leader wants to help. Active listening is one of the most powerful ways to build trust and help employees find meaning in their work.

Reflective listening is the third kind of listening, and it is also helpful in building trust. Reflective listening techniques are necessary when an employee presents a problem with an emotional component. Suppose, for example, that an employee complains about extreme work stress during the pandemic and shows emotions of anger, frustration, or sadness. The leader must deal with the employee's emotions first before using active listening techniques. Again, questions are more effective than declarative sentences. For example, the leader might ask the employee to sit and collect their thoughts before pursuing the core problem. Of course, the process ends with the same active listening question: "What can I do to help you with this problem?"

3. **Trust takes a long time to develop.** Trust is a complicated and fragile emotion. Trust increases in direct

relation to the frequency of meaningful interactions. Leaders can build trust over time by using effective communication techniques that have three basic elements: First, the leader must tell employees what needs to be done—that is, set performance expectations. Second, the leader needs to explain why the performance expectations are important. This is where the leader sets the context, by connecting employee performance to the achievement of the organization's vision. Third, the leader must explain the importance of each employee to the organization. When communications between and among leaders and staff includes these three elements, trust increases, which strengthens the employee engagement bond.

4.   **Trust can be weakened or broken easily.** On the other hand, if the leader is perceived as a person who limits important information, is not consistent with expectations, and has a hidden agenda, then trust is impossible. In this scenario, employees will not only become disengaged, they will also go into self-protection mode. Because trust is fragile, it can be broken easily. And once trust is broken, it is difficult to reestablish. In fact, if the trust bond is damaged significantly, the only solution to improved employee engagement and organizational performance is to replace the leadership.

5.   **Trust is the glue and the lubricant for sustainable success.** The easiest way to understand trust dynamics is to remember the essence of the trust bond. Quite simply, trust is "the benefit of the doubt." When strong trust bonds exist between and among employees and the leadership, there is some room for uncertainty. But if trust is low or nonexistent, then leadership communication will be met with skepticism: "I wonder what the real agenda is?" When the trust bond is strong, staff do not waste time looking for hidden agendas. Trust is the glue that

holds organizations together during uncertain and difficult times. The 2020 pandemic demonstrated the mastic power of trust. Healthcare providers worked exceptionally hard in an environment of pandemic uncertainty.

6. **Trust is different from likeability—there is no relationship between being liked and being trusted.** A person does not need to be liked to be trusted. While it may be easier to trust someone who is liked, it is not a requirement. It is possible to trust a cardiac surgeon to perform your operation even though you don't like the surgeon's personality. The key determinants of trust are honesty, openness, and consistency. If the leader possesses these leadership traits, then likeability or unlikability is much less important. In fact, a leader could be liked because of their personality but not trusted because they always seem to have a hidden agenda. The goal of all leaders should be to earn employees' trust and respect. Being liked is nice, but it should not be a leadership goal.

Profiles of Performance

Rear Admiral Anne Swap: Do Whatever Is in the Best Interest of the Patient

Rear Admiral Anne Swap, FACHE, is a US Navy flag officer who is responsible for the joint services healthcare delivery systems in the National Capital Market, Bethesda, Maryland. As a senior leader in the Defense Health Agency under the US Department of Defense, she is responsible for the provision of healthcare for more than 200,000 beneficiaries. Anne takes a multifaceted approach to fostering employee engagement. She understands the power of corporate values and an

(continued)

(continued from previous page)

inspirational vision. The values of honor, courage, and commitment underpin all her decisions about how to interact with her peers and her staff. Her inspirational, directional, and measurable vision is "to provide the same levels of care for all; to provide the best value within limited resources." Anne also has a motto: "To do whatever is in the best interest of the patient."

Her approach to engagement, especially during a pandemic, is focused on the organizational factors that contribute to her staff becoming demoralized. Anne's approach to working with staff during difficult times starts with reminding them why they chose to work in healthcare. Anne believes that healthcare delivery professionals have a special kind of courage.

She is very open, sharing problems and requesting help with solutions. Anne says that her personal leadership goal is to be seen as authentic. She asks herself, "What does it mean to serve?" The answer to this question drives her desire to be available to staff. "I try to never deprive people of my time. I show respect by sharing time." She is motivated to keep the organization aligned and everyone focused on the important work of delivering high-quality care. Finally, Anne states that "Healthcare is not an easy business, but it is about people, and people are very forgiving if you treat them like human beings."

SUMMARY

Meaningful work is the second of the three developmental and sequential steps to sustainable engagement. The first step is aligned values, the second step is finding meaning in work, and the final step is becoming part of a transcendent purpose. This chapter presented the factors that determine the amount of meaning employees find in their work. The critical factor that connects employees meaningfully to their jobs is the power of the corporate vision statement. A vision is a description of a desirable future. It is inspirational, directional, and measurable. It is the basis for strategy development, departmental plans, and, ultimately, the work of each employee. Ideally, all employees should be able draw a line from their tasks to the achievement of the departmental plan, the strategic plan, and the achievement of the vision.

Trust is a critical factor in converting the words of the vision into meaningful work. It serves as a bridge from a theoretical statement to a living document. Trust is the perception of honesty, openness, and reliability. It takes time to develop and can be broken easily. Leaders can build trust by using active listening techniques and by communicating in ways that show employees how corporate decisions affect them. Without trust, the vision statement will remain just a statement. Vision and trust are the best leadership tools to help employees find meaning in their work.

QUESTIONS FOR ASSESSMENT AND DISCUSSION

Thinking about your own organization, respond to the following statements on a scale of 1 to 5, where 5 = strongly agree, 4 = agree, 3 = uncertain, 2 = disagree, and 1 = strongly disagree.

Vision
1. Everyone knows their role in vision achievement.
2. Our vision drives our strategic and tactical plans.
3. We have a comprehensive vision communication plan for our staff and community.
4. Our staff development plans are based on the skills needed to achieve the vision.

5. The board agenda always includes a discussion of vision achievement metrics.

Trust
1. I encourage honest and open communication to flow from any direction.
2. I listen nonjudgmentally regardless of whether the information is good or bad.
3. I behave consistently.
4. I keep my promises.
5. I show genuine regard for others' knowledge, contributions, and experience.

REFERENCES

Amabile, T., and S. Kramer. 2012. "How Leaders Kill Meaning at Work." McKinsey and Company. Published January 1. www.mckinsey.com/featured-insights/leadership/how-leaders-kill-meaning-at-work.

Cable, D., and F. Vermeulen. 2018. "Making Work Meaningful: A Leader's Guide." McKinsey and Company. Published October 26. www.mckinsey.com/business-functions/organization/our-insights/making-work-meaningful-a-leaders-guide.

Covey, S. M. R. 2006. *The Speed of Trust: The One Thing That Changes Everything*. New York: Simon & Shuster.

Csikszentmihalyi, M. 1997. *Flow: The Psychology of Optimal Performance*. New York: Basic Books.

Fromm, E. 2019. "On Wisdom and the Meaning of Life." *Excellence Reporter*. Published May 28. https://excellencereporter.com/2019/05/28/erich-fromm-on-the-wisdom-and-the-meaning-of-life/.

Palmer, R., and B. Schaninger. 2018. "The Line Between Meaning and Organizational Health." McKinsey and Company. Published October 26. www.mckinsey.com/business-functions/organization/our-insights/the-link-between-meaning-and-organizational-health.

CHAPTER 4

The Purpose of Purpose

The purpose of life is a life of purpose.
—Robert Byrne

When you're surrounded by people who share a passionate commitment around a common purpose, anything is possible.
—Howard Schultz

Explore this next frontier where the boundaries between work and higher purpose are merging into one, where doing good is good for business.
—Richard Branson

MISSION CREATES CONNECTION TO GREATER PURPOSE

Sustainable employee engagement is firmly in place when *employees' values* and core *corporate values* are aligned; when employees find their work meaningful because of their connection to the organization's *vision*; and when employees see their daily tasks as part of a greater purpose because of their connection to the organization's *mission*. This developmental process creates the corporate culture necessary for work to become transcendent and for employees to become fully engaged. The organization's mission enables employees to move from doing meaningful work to being part of a greater purpose.

Mission statements explain, define, and demonstrate the organization's "reason for being." All successful organizations have three key components:

1. **Core values**—the beliefs that underpin our decisions. Core values connect employees to the organization: "I have a good job."
2. **Vision statement**—where we are headed. The vision provides meaningful work: "I have a career."
3. **Mission statement**—*why we exist*. The mission gives employees a purpose that transcends the job: "I have a calling."

Ask yourself—Do you have a job? A career? Or a calling?

WHAT IS THE PURPOSE OF PURPOSE?

The John Templeton Foundation (2018) discusses the psychology of purpose: "In psychological terms, a consensus definition for purpose has emerged in the literature according to which *purpose is a stable and generalized intention to accomplish something that is at once personally meaningful and at the same time leads to productive engagement with some aspect of the world beyond self.* Not all goals that are personally meaningful experiences contribute to purpose, but in the intersection of goal orientation, personal meaningfulness, and a focus beyond the self, a distinct conception of purpose emerges." The healthcare industry would seem to be a place where professionals could "accomplish something that is at once personally meaningful and . . . leads to productive engagement." Individuals who are attracted to the helping professions typically find purpose and meaning in the daily work of caring for others in their time of need. However, this inherent sense of worth that results from meaningful work is often diminished by the regulatory and financial pressures of working in healthcare. It doesn't need to be this way.

Amy Wrzesniewski, a professor at the Yale School of Management, has studied meaningful and purposeful work dynamics. Her research demonstrates the power of the hierarchy of job, meaningful work, and transcendent purpose. In a *Harvard Business Review* article, Wrzesniewski and Jane E. Dutton (2020, 1) describe "job crafting— changing your job to make it more engaging and meaningful." The authors go on: "The principles of job crafting remain deeply relevant in a world where job structure is rapidly changing, putting more and more responsibility on the individual for the experience and engagement in their work. While this certainly creates challenges, it also brings opportunities to build the kinds of tasks, relational, and cognitive landscapes that bring meaning to work" (5).

FINDING PURPOSE IN WORK BEGINS WITH THE ORGANIZATION'S MISSION

The mission is captured in a brief statement that describes why the organization exists—its fundamental purpose. The mission statement expresses the heart of the organization and its motivation for continued viability. It is important to understand the difference between the mission statement and the vision statement. The mission statement explains "why we exist," whereas the vision states "where we are going." Mission statements don't change. If an organization changes its mission, it change the company's purpose, and in fact, it creates a new company. A vision statement can change as needed to meet market, technological, and regulatory demands. And, of course, when the vision changes, new strategic and tactical plans, timelines, and metrics are necessary.

A 2020 McKinsey & Company report explains how an organization's mission statement is an expression of its purpose: "Purpose answers the question, 'What would the world lose if your company disappeared?' It defines the company's core reason for being and its resulting positive impact on the world. Winning companies are driven by purpose, reach higher for it, and achieve more because of it" (Leape, Zou, and Simpson 2020). The report details the "5Ps" of a purpose-driven organization: "Portfolio strategy and products; People and culture; Processes and systems; Performance metrics; and Positions and engagement." The applications of the 5Ps of a purpose-driven organization to the healthcare industry and the implications for trustees and executives are significant. The critical decisions made by healthcare trustees and executives should always be guided by the question, "What would the world lose if your company (healthcare delivery system) disappeared?" Each strategic and financial decision should have to pass the "mission statement test." That is, does this decision reinforce the organization's reason for existence? Or, does this decision weaken our purpose in any way? If a decision is driven by the organization's mission and purpose, the governance body should make it a policy, and executives should deliver the product or service. However, if a decision is made for reasons other than strengthening the mission and purpose—for example, to satisfy a disruptive physician—then the decision is wrong.

The organization's vision statement provides meaning, while the mission statement provides a transcendent purpose. Assuming that employee and organizational values are aligned, sustainable engagement can be achieved by creating a culture in which employees see their efforts as progress toward achieving the vision and believe that their work is an essential part of the mission—the reason the organization exists and its purpose for being.

The following are some examples of healthcare mission statements and vision statements. Notice the qualitative difference—the mission statement describes why the organization exists, and the vision statement describes where the organization is headed.

- **Scripps Health, La Jolla, California**—President/CEO Chris Van Gorder (profiled at the end of this chapter)
  - "*The Scripps mission is simple and heartfelt:* Scripps strives to provide superior health services in a caring

environment and to make a positive, measurable difference in the health of individuals in the communities we serve.

We devote our resources to delivering quality, safe, cost-effective, socially responsible health care services. We advance clinical research, community health education, education of physicians and health care professionals and sponsor graduate medical education.

We collaborate with others to deliver a continuum of care that improves the health of our community."

— *Scripps Vision:* "Scripps Health will continue to be the leading health care delivery system in the greater San Diego community, as evidenced by the highest clinical quality, patient safety, and patient, physician and employee satisfaction. This will be achieved through unending focus on patient-centered and compassionate care, cost-effective operations, research, advanced technology and innovation."

- **Dartmouth-Hitchcock Health, Lebanon, New Hampshire**—Karen Clements, Chief Nursing Officer (see profile in chapter 10)
  - *Mission:* "We advance health through research, education, clinical practice and community partnerships, providing each person the best care, in the right place, at the right time, every time."
  - *Vision:* "To achieve the healthiest population possible, leading the transformation of health care in our region and setting the standard for our nation."
- **Baptist Health, Fort Smith, Arkansas**—Kim Miller, President/CEO (also profiled in chapter 10)
  - *Mission:* "Baptist health exists to provide quality patient services, promote and protect the voluntary not-for-profit healthcare system, provide quality health education and respond to the changing needs of Arkansans with Christian compassion and personal concern."

- *Vision:* "Baptist Health will improve the health of Arkansans by changing the way healthcare is delivered."
- **UW Health, Madison, Wisconsin**—Alan Kaplan, CEO (see profile in chapter 7)
  - *Mission:* "Advancing health without compromise through: Service; Scholarship; Science; Social Responsibility."
  - *Vision:* "Remarkable Healthcare."

These organizations and the leaders showcased in the Profiles of Performance, as well as others mentioned in this book, are models of excellence in aligning corporate values and employee values. Doing so makes it possible to customize the work so that employees can see how their tasks are meaningful. They can see how their efforts help achieve the organization's vision, and the organizational mission helps employees achieve purpose in their work. In other words, employees understand that their work is a calling—a socially valuable contribution—even if the specific tasks involved are not always pleasant.

Finding ourselves, and being sure of the reason why we are in this world, is a basic human drive. While this process is mostly subconscious, we are always deciding what we want to do with our existence, which leads us all to the same point—we want to succeed, we want to make a difference, and we want our lives to have meaning and a worthwhile purpose. In the work environment, every worker, and every task performed, should result in a sense of meaning and provide a purpose greater than the paycheck.

Martin Seligman, a professor of psychology at the University of Pennsylvania, developed a theory called "positive psychology" that attempts to explain the complex dynamics of happiness in our daily lives. Seligman posits that happiness comprises three dimensions that can be cultivated (Fisk 2020):

1. **The Pleasant Life**—positive emotions and pleasure . . . feeling more

2. **The Good Life**—togetherness and engagement . . .
contributing more
3. **The Meaningful life**—fulfilment and meaning . . .
achieving more

Seligman's theory provides a useful model for healthcare leaders to create sustainable employee engagement through aligned values, meaningful tasks, and purposeful contributions. Seligman identifies five elements of what he calls "authentic happiness," which are captured by the abbreviation "PERMA": positive emotion, engagement, relationship, meaning, and accomplishment.

Seligman (2002, 10) believes that positive emotion is the most obvious connection to happiness: "Positive Psychology takes seriously the bright hope that if you find yourself stuck in the parking lot of life, with few and only ephemeral pleasures, with minimal gratifications, without meaning, there is a road out. This road takes you through the countryside of pleasure and graduation, up into the high country of strength and virtue, and finally to the peaks of lasting fulfillment: meaning and purpose."

Healthcare workers around the world suffered great stress during the COVID-19 pandemic, and they continue to be stressed in the emerging post-pandemic world. However, we have heard daily stories of the exceptional work and the heroism of frontline workers. Reports of total exhaustion were accompanied by statements of personal meaning and workers finding a greater purpose in treating the very sick patients. Positive emotion is not always the result of pleasure. It happens when one is totally connected to one's life purpose.

Seligman's second element of happiness is engagement. He believes that "activities that meet our need for engagement flood our body with positive neurotransmitters and hormones that elevate one's sense of well-being. This engagement helps us remain present, as well as synthesize the activities where we find calm, focus, and joy" (Fisk 2020). Seligman's description of the need for engagement is one of the main underpinnings of this book. In chapter 1,

I discussed the erosion of healthcare workers' sense of well-being. Finding joy among healthcare workers is a rare discovery indeed. The role that engagement plays in an individual's life and the contribution that engagement makes to long-term corporate success cannot be overstated.

The third element in Seligman's theory is relationships. "Relationships and social connections are crucial to meaningful lives . . . We thrive on connections that promote love, intimacy, and strong emotional and physical interactions with other humans" (Fisk 2020). Once again, data from the COVID-19 pandemic lend strong support to Seligman's theory of the importance of relationships. The pandemic required many individuals to self-isolate. Weddings were canceled. Funerals were held without family members in attendance. Holidays were spent alone or with a small group of members of one's "bubble." Children were faced with distance learning. And, no one was shaking hands or hugging!

In a study conducted for the Kaiser Family Foundation, Nirmita Panchal and colleagues (2021) found that during the COVID-19 pandemic and the economic crisis it precipitated, "about 4 in 10 adults nationwide . . . reported symptoms of anxiety or depressive disorder—a four-fold increase from pre-pandemic levels." These negative realities of the pandemic require that healthcare leaders be extra-sensitive to the mental as well as physical stresses that employees are experiencing. Seligman suggests that a possible antidote to the deleterious effects of the pandemic is to support relationship time, for example, through small-group catharsis sessions, daily celebrations, social media postings about successes, or anything that supports workers' need for positive relationships.

Seligman's fourth element of authentic happiness is meaning: "Having an answer as to 'why we are on this earth?' is a key ingredient that can drive us towards fulfillment" (Fisk 2020). Meaning is tied closely with the final element of happiness—accomplishment. Together, meaning and accomplishment create a life with purpose—or, as Seligman believes, *authentic happiness.*

The answer to the question "what is the purpose of purpose?" is authentic happiness. This raises another question: What can health-care leaders do to make the organization's mission come alive for employees in a way that their work has a transcendent purpose? The answer can be found in the skills associated with the theory of emotional intelligence.

LEADERSHIP SKILL FOR CREATING PURPOSE: EMOTIONAL INTELLIGENCE

Howard Gardner is a professor at Harvard University. In his 1983 book *Frames of Mind: The Theory of Multiple Intelligences*, Gardner introduced the notion that there is more to human intelligence than IQ. His work challenged the belief that a single score is sufficient to account for intelligence. In fact, Gardner identified seven different types of intelligence:

1. **Linguistic intelligence**—the ability to understand the meaning and order of words. Think about people who speak multiple languages.

2. **Logical-mathematical intelligence**—the ability to understand the complex order of things. Think about mathematicians, chemists, physicists.

3. **Musical intelligence**—the ability to write, sing, and play music. Think about the "three Bs" of classical music—Bach, Beethoven, and Brahms.

4. **Spatial intelligence**—the ability to think in three-dimensional forms and pictures. Think about architects.

5. **Bodily-kinesthetic intelligence**—the ability to move and control one's body movements. Think about gymnasts.

6. **Interpersonal intelligence**—the ability to perceive and understand others. Think about therapists, religious leaders, and some politicians.

7. **Intrapersonal intelligence**—the ability to understand one's emotions and feelings. Think of novelists, life coaches, and highly effective parents.

Psychologist and science journalist Daniel Goleman added an eighth intelligence to this list. In his 1995 book *Emotional Intelligence: Why It Can Matter More Than IQ*, Goleman introduced the concept of emotional intelligence, or the ability to manage oneself and one's relationships effectively. Goleman initially outlined four components of emotional intelligence:

1. **Self-awareness**—the ability to know one's emotions, strengths, and weaknesses.
2. **Self-management**—the ability to be flexible depending on the situation and to be able to control one's positive and negative emotions.
3. **Social awareness**—the ability to understand someone else's point of view, to show empathy, and to adapt to a changing social context.
4. **Relationship management**—the ability to engage and inspire others and to deal with conflict in a mature way.

Goleman later expanded the number of components of emotional intelligence. In an article for the *Harvard Business Review*, Goleman (1998, 95) laid out five components of emotional intelligence at work:

1. **Self-awareness**—the ability to recognize and understand your moods, emotions, and drives, as well as their effects on others.
2. **Self-regulation**—the ability to redirect disruptive impulses and moods; a propensity to suspend judgment—to think before acting.

3. **Motivation**—a passion to work for reasons that go beyond money or status; a propensity to pursue goals with energy and persistence.

4. **Empathy**—the ability to understand the emotional makeup of other people; skill in treating people according to their emotional reactions.

5. **Social skill**—proficiency in managing relationships and building networks; an ability to find common ground and build rapport.

The most effective healthcare leaders, regardless of title or place in the organizational hierarchy, display these components of emotional intelligence. Emotionally intelligent supervisors, managers, directors, and senior executives manifest the most important characteristic of all the organizational intangibles—that is, the ability to convert the organization's mission into a belief in its transcendent purpose. This ability is the foundation for a sustainable bond of employee engagement. The most common traits of leaders who embody emotional intelligence are trustworthiness, comfort with uncertainty, a strong drive to achieve, cross-cultural understanding, positive inclusiveness, self-confidence, and, perhaps most important, optimism—even when confronted with failure. These leaders typically have high IQs, but also, more importantly, high emotional intelligence. Goleman (1995, 16) makes an important point: "CEOs are hired for their intellect and business expertise and fired for their lack of emotional intelligence." To be clear, this statement by no means diminishes the importance of high intellect. Leaders need to be very intelligent. However, Goleman notes that high intellect without high emotional intelligence is not enough to inspire others. Goleman speculates that "as much as 80% of adult success comes from Emotional Intelligence."

Finally, Goleman's theory of emotional intelligence has one characteristic that Gardner's seven intelligences do not possess: the ability to increase the level of intelligence by systematically improving the components. For example, the degree to which an individual possesses each of Gardner's seven intelligences is, in theory, fixed at birth. No matter how much one tries, the intelligence will remain the same. However, emotional intelligence can be developed by focusing on actions such as taking personal surveys to increase self-knowledge; working on patience to increase self-management; studying and practicing team building to increase social management skills; and working on listening and empathy to increase the ability to read group dynamics. The theoretical model created by Goleman and expanded by many researchers and practitioners has tremendous potential to help healthcare leaders create a transcendent purpose for employee engagement.

Profiles of Performance

Chris Van Gorder: Building Partnerships with Physicians

Chris Van Gorder, FACHE, is the president and CEO of Scripps Health System in La Jolla, California. In his 21-year tenure as the leader of Scripps Health, the organization has grown from a system with just under $1 billion in annual revenue and 10,000 employees to a system with more than $3 billion in revenue, more than 15,000 employees, and over 3,000 affiliated physicians. Under Chris's leadership, Scripps Health has made *Fortune* magazine's "100 Best Companies to Work For" list for 12 years in a row. In terms of quality healthcare, Scripps has been named to both the *US News & World Report* Best Hospitals list and the Truven Health Analytics "100 Top Hospitals" list for several years. While these facts are impressive, the real story is how Chris led the amazing transformation.

Chris is a true servant leader. He began his career at Scripps Health as the interim chief operating officer in 1999. Five months after starting work at Scripps Health, he replaced a

(continued)

(continued from previous page)

CEO who had overseen a $15 million a year loss and such poor physician relations that he received a vote of no confidence. In 1999, the organization was bleeding red ink, physician confidence had hit bottom, and staff turnover was high. Through this morass of negative organizational dynamics, Chris began to engineer a path to excellence. Chris's leadership style can be described with the following words: transparent, collaborative, talent finder, inclusive, culture warrior, team builder, compassionate, and chief culture officer.

Chris started the organizational transformation by building partnerships with the physician leaders. He began the process of building trust by creating a new Physician Leadership Cabinet. The stated tangible purpose of the Physician Leadership Cabinet was to create a platform for Chris and the physicians to determine the best way to provide care with scarce resources. The unstated intangible purpose was to build trust between and among the physicians and executives. The cabinet was formed more than 20 years ago. It continues today, as Chris states, as "a forum for us to run this company together."

After initiating a process to improve relationships between physicians and executives, Chris turned to the corporate culture. His plan is anchored in a series of "Leadership Academies." He started with the belief that culture strengthening takes 5 to 10 years. The Leadership Academy is a year-long program for 25 high-potential leaders. The graduates of this program become the leaders of culture change. The program has been successfully producing "Scripps Culture Change Leaders" for 20 years.

The latest Scripps employee engagement survey was completed in the midst of the COVID-19 pandemic. The results showed a 5% increase over the previous—already quite

(continued)

(continued from previous page)

high—results. The survey vendor told Chris that they had never seen such gains, regardless of the pandemic.

Chris says that *"What* a leader does is important, but long-term success happens only when the *why* and *how* are explained often and in the most transparent ways."

SUMMARY

Purpose-driven performance is the third and highest form of employee engagement. A prerequisite for purpose-driven performance is the alignment of personal and corporate values. Once values are aligned, the specific tasks required of each employee must be meaningful and tied directly to the achievement of the organization's vision. Then, and only then, can the organization's mission be the platform for purposeful work. Purpose creates a transcendent bond between the employee's job and the organization's purpose. The most important trait for healthcare leaders seeking to create a corporate culture in which the organization's mission underpins all behavior is emotional intelligence—the ability to know oneself, to be self-disciplined, to build teams, and to manage group behavior. Emotional intelligence is the only one of the eight intelligences that can be improved—the others are fixed.

QUESTIONS FOR ASSESSMENT AND DISCUSSION

Thinking about your own organization, respond to the following statements on a scale of 1 to 5, where 5 = strongly agree, 4 = agree, 3 = uncertain, 2 = disagree, and 1 = strongly disagree.

1. Our mission defines our reason for being.
2. Our mission helps us understand what the community would be like if we did not exist.

3. We are transparent when discussing "why" we are doing something.

4. Our employees feel they are a part of something important—something bigger than themselves.

5. The mission, values, and vision are used at the governance, executive, and department levels to determine the quality of a decision.

REFERENCES

Dutton, J. E., and A. Wrzesniewski. 2020. "What Job Crafting Looks Like." *Harvard Business Review*. Published March 12. https://hbr.org/2020/03/what-job-crafting-looks-like.

Fisk, P. 2020. "The Psychology of Happiness." Gamechanger. Published February 27. www.peterfisk.com/2020/02/the-psychology-of-happiness-authentic-happiness-is-about-more-than-pleasure-it-requires-engagement-and-a-sense-of-purpose-too/.

Gardner, H. 1983. *Frames of Mind: The Theory of Multiple Intelligences*. New York: Basic Books.

Goleman, D. 1995. *Emotional Intelligence: Why It Can Matter More Than IQ*. New York: Bantam Books.

———. 1998. "What Makes a Leader?" *Harvard Business Review* 76 (6): 93–102.

John Templeton Foundation. 2018. "The Psychology of Purpose." Accessed April 23, 2021. www.templeton.org/discoveries/the-psychology-of-purpose.

Leape, S., J. Zou, and B. Simpson. 2020. "More Than a Mission Statement: How the 5Ps Embed Purpose to Deliver Value." McKinsey & Company. Published November 5.

www.mckinsey.com/business-functions/strategy-and-corporate-finance/our-insights/more-than-a-mission-statement-how-the-5ps-embed-purpose-to-deliver-value.

Panchal, N., R. Kamal, C. Cox, and R. Garfield. 2021. "The Implications of COVID-19 for Mental Health and Substance Abuse." Kaiser Family Foundation. Published February 10. www.kff.org/coronavirus-covid-19/issue-brief/the-implications-of-covid-19-for-mental-health-and-substance-use/.

Seligman, M. E. P. 2002. *Authentic Happiness: Using the New Positive Psychology to Realize Your Potential for Lasting Fulfillment.* New York: Free Press.

CHAPTER 5

Motivation and Engagement

You'll never change your life until you change something you do daily. The secret of your success is found in your daily routine.
—John C. Maxwell

I have not failed. I've just found 10,000 ways that won't work.
—Thomas Edison

Passion is energy. Feel the power that comes from focusing on what excites you.
—Oprah Winfrey

UNLEASHING EMPLOYEE MOTIVATION

Have you ever heard an executive or manager say any of the following? "My staff are not motivated." "We need to motivate the staff more." "If only we could pay the staff more, they would be more motivated." All of these statements are incorrect and demonstrate a poor understanding of the fundamentals of human motivation. Most motivational theories posit that all people are 100 percent motivated, 100 percent of the time. As a leader, you can only unleash, guide, and direct human motivation. You cannot increase it or decrease it. Motivation is always driving a person's behavior.

When you hear a manager say, "My staff are not motivated," what that really means is that the employees are not motivated to do what the manager wants them to do. But they are 100 percent motivated—they are motivated to come to work late, take long lunch breaks, and do just enough work to get paid! Executives and managers may also exclaim, "I've tried everything to motivate my staff!" Once again, there is a basic falsehood in this statement: It is executives and managers who are responsible for creating a work environment—that is, a strong corporate culture—that unleashes, guides, and directs staff motivation and performance toward departmental goals, not staff. The last and perhaps most common misconception about human motivation has to do with the importance of money in unleashing and directing motivation. Money is a terrible long-term motivator.

The role that money plays in motivating workers will be discussed in more detail later in this chapter. The short version is that money demotivates employees in two ways and motivates in only one way. Money demotivates employees if the amount is perceived by the receiver as too little. And, interestingly, money also demotivates employees if it is perceived as very high. When the money is perceived as very high, the recipient often becomes reluctant to do anything that might result in the loss of the desired amount money. In these cases, innovation is stifled, and risk avoidance becomes the modus operandi. You may hear a senior executive say, "Let's not do anything to rock the boat." In other words: "I've got a good pay and benefit package, and I don't want to lose it!"

Money works to motivate employees only when the amount is perceived as fair. But just try to define "fair"—it's a moving target. Suppose an individual or a group receives a 3 percent pay increase: If a 2 percent raise was expected, the amount will be perceived as fair and therefore motivating. But if a 4 percent raise was expected, the amount will be perceived as unfair and therefore demotivating.

COMMON THEORIES OF MOTIVATION

What is motivation? In its most basic form, motivation is a concept about individual needs and how each individual fulfills those needs. But motivational theory goes beyond needs. Because motivation is about more than the fulfillment of individual needs, it is impossible for anyone to motivate someone else. Rather, the leader's role is to create an environment that unleashes each individual's motivation in a way that ensures that staff needs, wants, and desires are fulfilled. This takes us back to the importance of aligned values, meaningful vision, focused work, and mission-based transcendent purpose.

Motivation is a personal dynamic that inspires and directs behavior. In terms of engagement at work, all workers are motivated to some degree. The relationship between the worker and the work tasks determines the amount of motivation that drives each worker. We all have a capacity to perform. We all have needs that we want to satisfy at work. Variation in the capacity to perform is an important factor to consider when thinking about the amount of motivation and engagement that each employee possesses. A highly motivated person has a large capacity for performance, in comparison with someone with a lower capacity. Think of two glasses—one contains 20 ounces and the other contains 8 ounces. The lesson for healthcare leaders is that the individual's capacity cannot be changed—it is impossible, and just unreasonable, to expect workers to exceed their motivational capacity. In other words, don't try to pour 20 ounces of liquid into an 8-ounce glass!

Misunderstandings about the nature of human motivation are illustrated by the "Peter Principle." Adam Hayes (2021) explains that according to the Peter Principle, "employees rise up through a firm's hierarchy through promotion until they reach a level of respective incompetence. As a result . . . every position will eventually be filled by employees who are incompetent to fulfill the job duties of their respective positive positions." The important lesson for healthcare leaders is to avoid "one-size-fits-all" approaches to employee engagement. Leaders must understand that each employee has unique talents, skills, and motivational capacity.

Theoretical models have some useful applications to increasing employee engagement in healthcare. Abraham Maslow's hierarchy of needs was discussed in chapter 2. According to Maslow's motivational theory, someone who is hungry (a basic need) will be more motivated to find food than to find a transcendent purpose (a higher-level need). Higher-level needs can only be achieved after an individual's lower-level or basic needs are satisfied. The COVID-19 pandemic provided many opportunities to apply Maslow's hierarchy of needs. Direct care providers, ancillary healthcare personnel, and business professionals were all physically and emotionally stretched beyond their normal ability to cope. Emotional stress and physical exhaustion were common results of the pressures of the pandemic. Within such an environment, a manager was more likely to hear "I'm just trying to get through the day without getting sick" than "I'm seeking self-actualization." For much of the pandemic, workers with school-age children needed to stay at home to supervise distance learning, exacerbating their work stress. The most empathic healthcare leaders were aware of the internal and external pressures on employees and responded by creating flexible scheduling options and offering in-hospital "relief rooms" for workers.

Another motivational theory that has utility for healthcare leaders is behaviorist theory, which is primarily associated with the American psychologist B. F. Skinner. Skinner (1938) introduced a process called behavior modification. He believed that human performance is controlled to a large degree by positive and negative reinforcement. Behavior modification is based on four "schedules" of reinforcement: fixed ratio, variable ratio, fixed interval, and variable interval. A fixed-ratio schedule means that the individual receives reinforcement after demonstrating the desired behavior a fixed number of times. Piecework is an example of a fixed-ratio schedule. A variable ratio means that the reinforcement is unpredictable. Gambling on slot machines is a variable-ratio schedule design. One never knows how many times the machine must be played before there is a payout. A fixed-interval schedule of reinforcement means that the reinforcement is delivered over a specific time period, regardless of the individual's performance. Paychecks are delivered over a uniform period—for example, every two weeks. A variable-interval schedule means that the time between reinforcements is unknown—it varies. Skinner's behavior modification theory is useful when considering how to reward staff for special effort. A detailed discussion of this theory in relation to money is presented later in this chapter.

One final thought about behavior modification: Punishment is also a part of behaviorism. Punishment is anything that follows a behavior that decreases the probability of that behavior happening again. For example, suppose a supervisor yells at a subordinate to stop doing something. The individual who is on the receiving end of the punishment will stop the behavior. However, punishment is much more complex. First, punishment only works as long as the *threat* of punishment exists. As soon as the threat of punishment is removed, the behavior will return, and it may even increase. In the previous example, the employee will stop the offending behavior only as long as the supervisor is present. When the coast is clear, the subordinate will likely continue the behavior. Second, punishment tends to elicit anger and other negative emotions in the person being punished. Mutual respect, trust, commitment, engagement, and other positive drivers of a high-performance organization cannot exist in a punitive work environment.

A motivational theory that is more focused on work and employees was created by psychologist Frederick Herzberg (1976). It is called the "motivation-hygiene theory" or the "two-factor theory." Herzberg's theory is divided into two parts: *Satisfiers and dissatisfiers* is the first part, and *motivation maintenance* is the second part.

The first part of Herzberg's theory posits that the factors that make a job satisfying (satisfiers) are different from the factors that make it dissatisfying (dissatisfiers). For example, giving staff more money may create less dissatisfaction, but it will not lead to sustainable job satisfaction. Sustainable job satisfaction is a function of employees working on tasks that are intrinsically rewarding.

The second part of Herzberg's theory, motivation maintenance, holds that certain factors are used to keep employees from becoming unhappy. For example, an employee might be satisfied with a pay increase, but six months later, that employee might be looking for another raise. Herzberg believes that the absence of perceived fairness in pay and benefits will always make employees dissatisfied, but pay increases will not necessarily make them happier or more productive.

A final motivational theory that has utility for healthcare leaders who wish to create an environment of sustainable engagement is called "personal investment." In their 1986 book *The Motivation Factor: A Theory of Personal Investment*, Martin L. Maehr and Larry A. Braskamp focus on adult motivation, especially in the work environment. Their basic theory is that humans are internally motivated to work on tasks that have the most meaning to them. This theory is based on Maehr and Braskamp's research, which showed that when workers are free to do anything, they choose to invest their time and energy in the tasks they consider most important. Personal investment is a theory of intrinsic motivation. When this concept is extended to work, it suggests that when a task diverges from what the individual considers to be important, the need for external motivators (e.g., money, threats) to achieve the task is greater. When the task is closer to what the employee considers important, it is more likely that the individual will have strong internal motivation and little (if any) need for external motivators. The implication for healthcare leaders is to involve staff in the delineation of tasks to increase their personal investment (i.e., their internal motivation) in performance.

Another useful concept from Maehr and Braskamp's theory of personal investment is that all adults possess four motivational drivers to different degrees: recognition, accomplishment, power, and affiliation. The degree to which these motivational factors are present determines the best way to activate an employee's internal motivators. The factors of recognition and accomplishment determine whether a worker is internally or externally motivated.

The factors of power and affiliation determine whether a worker is individualistic or team oriented. Employees who have high recognition needs will respond to external motivators such as compliments, pay for performance, and public recognition. However, external motivators will not work as well with employees who are driven by accomplishment—and they may even have a negative impact on motivation. High achievers are best motivated by challenges that stretch their current level of performance. Workers who have high power needs tend to prefer to work alone, and they may be fairly competitive with their peers. However, workers with high affiliation needs are highly socialized and prefer to work on team-oriented projects.

These four factors explain why it may be difficult to form teams of physicians, who typically are motivated by high accomplishment and high power. It also explains why external rewards work well with younger professionals, who tend to have high recognition needs because of their relative inexperience. Younger and newer staff require much more feedback than seasoned staff. In essence, Maehr and Braskamp's personal investment theory supports the notion that a one-size-fits-all approach to employee engagement is likely to fail and may even backfire.

MONEY AS A MOTIVATOR: MYTHS AND REALITIES

Money is a poor, short-term motivator at best, and at worst it is demotivating. A common myth is that the paycheck is a motivator. You might hear a manager say, "I don't know why they are not motivated, they get paid, don't they?" The paycheck is not a motivator—it is an entitlement. Remember Skinner's schedules of reinforcement. A paycheck is received at fixed intervals. That means the employee gets a check every two weeks, regardless of performance. The problem with using money on a fixed-interval schedule is that it becomes an expectation. Employees feel they are owed a paycheck. In fact, employees use personal pronouns when talking about their paycheck: "When will I get *my* money?" If you want to test this notion, randomly select a paycheck and short the check by $1. You will most likely hear, in a short amount of time, "You shorted my check. I want my money."

If you want to use money as a motivator, it cannot be given more than once for a particular behavior. The best example of an industry that uses money as a motivator is gambling. Think about Las Vegas: People are consistently motivated to continue gambling over long periods of time, even when they have incurred significant losses. They continue betting in the hope of getting a big return based on probability theory—"My luck has got to change." Skinner's variable-ratio schedule explains why people continue gambling. They never know when the game will pay off! The unpredictability of the variable schedule maximizes motivation.

Fact: When money is predictable, it is not motivating; it is an entitlement. The only time a paycheck is motivating is when employees fear the loss of it. Consider, for example, the group behavior of a labor union if it believes that a new contract will decrease employees' benefits. Union members will protest increases in healthcare premiums, because that takes money out of their paychecks. Fear of the loss of money is a powerful negative motivator.

Pay and benefits often rank last or near the bottom on lists of employee motivators. Robert Tanner (2021) identifies the top five employee motivators in his research:

1. Challenging work
2. Recognition
3. Employee involvement
4. Job security
5. Compensation

Tanner's conclusion is that if you "want to motivate your employees," then "give them fair pay, job security, a chance to succeed, and recognition for their accomplishments."

Likewise, Melanie Holly Pasch (2019) concludes that "money is not a long-term motivator." She explains that once high salaries and bonuses are given,

> They become part of employee expectations for the coming year. Expectations climb and if a company fails to keep up, the disappointment combined with the financial cost may not be the best strategy at least in terms of employee engagement. Providing competitive salaries and bonuses is still a must, but don't make the mistake of thinking high pay will keep employees at your company longer. Money may be a motivator in getting people to accept your offer and join your company, but money is not a long-term motivator in terms of performance.

Pasch notes that "for 80% of the working population the money is not the lever that leads to engagement and buy in. Workers want to feel emotionally connected to the mission and service of the organization and to the customers they serve."

There is very little relationship between the amount of money staff receive and the degree of pride, loyalty, ownership, and engagement they demonstrate. A core principle of this book is that the degree to which money is used as a motivator is correlated with the degree of internal motivation. Sustainable performance has less to do with money and more to do with three factors: "I am valued," "I have clear role expectations," and "I have a future with this company." Any short-term spike in performance resulting from the use of money will last only a few weeks—and then staff who are motivated primarily by money will want more to produce the same effort.

Leaders can recognize high performance through nonmonetary compensation. The best way for leaders to reinforce high performers is captured by the abbreviation "SPINS":

1. **SP**ecific
2. **I**mmediate

3. Novel

4. Sincere

Healthcare leaders who are trusted and respected by employees respond positively to SPINS. Research suggests that employee engagement is driven more by intangible factors than by money and other tangibles. (See the profile of Michael Mayo of Baptist Health at the end of this chapter for a great example of how he uses SPINS.)

An apocryphal but educational story describes the role of money versus employee development: A CFO goes to the CEO and says, "I have some bad news and some good news." The CEO says, "Give me the bad news first." The CFO replies, "The company is bleeding red ink and losing a lot of money. But the good news is that if we cut one line item out of the budget, we will instantly go from red ink to black ink." The CEO asks what that line item pays for. The CFO says that eliminating the employee professional development budget will immediately make the company profitable. The CEO asks, "Why would we do that?" The CFO responds, "Why would we develop our employees when they might just leave?" The CEO thinks for a minute and responds, "What if we don't professionally develop our employees, *and they stay*?!"

Profiles of Performance

Michael Mayo: "We Are in the People Business"

Michael Mayo, DHA, FACHE, is the president and CEO of Baptist Health in Northeast Florida. One of the system's hospitals, Baptist Medical Center (BMC) in Jacksonville, is a 489-bed tertiary and regional referral center that is a part of a five-hospital, $2.5 billion health system. Thanks to Michael's

(continued)

(continued from previous page)

leadership over the last 10 years, BMC was named one of the "100 Top Hospitals for 2017" by Truven Health Analytics; one of *Becker's Hospital Review*'s "100 Great Hospitals in America" and *US News & World Report*'s "Best Hospitals" in 2020; and the number-one hospital in Jacksonville, as well as the number-four hospital in the state of Florida. Michael is a Fellow and an active member of the American College of Healthcare Executives, serving on the Council of Regents from 2017 to 2019 and elected to the Board of Governors in 2019.

Michael's long history of leading successful organizations gives him a cogent picture of employee engagement today compared with the past. "It was different years ago because we weren't in such a hurry. Today there are multiple productivity metrics that drive clinical performance. Also, the current structure seems to move the patient further from their physician." Michael goes on: "The role of the physician leader continues to emerge as an essential part of our engagement strategy. The hospital places a strong emphasis on physician leadership development. We believe that physician leaders can assist significantly in improving the connectedness of our team members and the delivery of high-quality care."

Michael has embedded a number motivational factors that increase employee engagement into BMC's corporate culture. He is guided by a strong personal belief: "We are in the people business. No technology, robotics, or other physical factors should get in the way of people taking care of people." Four "non-negotiable" principles support his belief in the importance of team members:

- **Respect**—in terms of caring for patients and their families. All team members are essential, whether they provide direct care or business support for

(continued)

(continued from previous page)

the care providers. Michael believes that mutual respect is the foundation for the team members' connectedness to their patient care mission.

- **Transparency**—team members need to be aware of every aspect of the organization that affects their work.

- **Presence**—Michael believes that as the hospital's CEO, he and the other BMC leaders must be seen. Tom Peters labeled this behavior in 1982 as "MBWA"—management by walking about. Michael is a model of MBWA and believes that leaders must lead by example. Leaders must be approachable.

- **Truthfulness**—Michael believes that it is vital that he and other hospital leaders be honest, open, and consistent in their messaging.

Michael's formula for sustainable team members is the sum of these four elements. When hospital leaders are respectful, transparent, present, and truthful, there is a much better chance that team members will find meaning in their work and a transcendent purpose in contributing to the organization's mission.

Michael displays one particularly unique behavior as he implements his version of SPINS (specific, immediate, novel, and sincere) to recognize excellent performance. He carries specially designed BMC "challenge coins" with him on his rounds (exhibit 5.1). A challenge coin is a small coin or medallion bearing an organization's emblem and originally given to an organization's members to prove membership when challenged. They traditionally are presented in recognition of special achievement. Michael gives them to employees who display one or more of BMC's core values.

Exhibit 5.1

SUMMARY

Motivation is a complex human characteristic. All humans are 100 percent motivated, 100 percent of the time. To say that "my employees are not motivated" is incorrect. Employees are motivated—but they may not motivated to do what you would like them to do. The main responsibility of the healthcare leader is to unleash, guide, and direct motivation. The best way to do this is for the leader to build a strong relationship with employees based on honesty, openness, and consistency. The leader must be viewed as authentic and as someone who cares about employees' personal and professional development. Of course, employee engagement starts with employees' perception that their pay and benefits are fair. But engagement is not based on pay and benefits beyond perceived fairness. Engagement is based on employees feeling respected, challenged, and connected to the organization's purpose.

What and how employees are motivated has been the subject of research for many years. The relative importance of intrinsic, values-based motivation versus extrinsic motivation based on monetary and other external rewards has long been debated. This chapter attempted to show that intrinsic, values-based motivators are the best drivers of sustainable employee engagement. Money and other external rewards can produce the desired level of productivity—for a short period of time. However, intrinsic, values-based motivation is self-sustaining. The use of negative motivators or punishments may produce a short-term increase in the desired behavior, but the long-term negative effects will ultimately weaken, and possibly destroy, worker motivation.

QUESTIONS FOR ASSESSMENT AND DISCUSSION

1. Has our budget for professional development increased or decreased over the last five years?
2. Is our employee pay and benefit package considered fair for our market?
3. Do our senior executives and middle managers practice MBWA—management by walking about?
4. Is the SPINS method used to reinforce high performance?
5. Does our board of trustees receive periodic data on employee engagement and the organization's approach to sustainable engagement?

REFERENCES

Hayes, A. 2021. "What Is the Peter Principle?" Investopedia. Published March 20. www.investopedia.com/terms/p/peter-principle.asp.

Herzberg, F. 1976. *The Managerial Choice: To Be Efficient and to Be Human*. Homewood, IL: Dow Jones-Irwin.

Maehr, M. L., and L. A. Braskamp. 1986. *The Motivation Factor: A Theory of Personal Investment*. Lexington, MA: Lexington Books.

Pasch, M. H. 2019. "Does Money Motivate? Employee Engagement and Compensation." Gloat. Published June 10. www. gloat.com/blog/does-money-motivate-employee-engagement-compensation/.

Skinner, B. F. 1938. *The Behavior of Organisms: An Experimental Analysis*. New York: Appleton-Century.

Tanner, R. 2021. "Top 5 Employee Motivators." Management Is a Journey. Published January 29. https://managementisajourney. com/fascinating-numbers-top-5-employee-motivators/.

CHAPTER 6

The Importance of Corporate Culture

If you get culture right, most of the other stuff will take care of itself.
—Tony Hsieh

Culture eats strategy for breakfast.
—Peter Drucker

Culture isn't just one aspect of the game—it is the game.
In the end, an organization is nothing more than the
collective capacity of its people to create value.
—Lou Gerstner

WHAT IS CORPORATE CULTURE
AND WHY IS IT IMPORTANT?

Edgar Schein is widely considered the "father of corporate culture." According to Schein (2017, 12), culture is "the deeper level of basic assumptions and beliefs that are shared by members of the organization that operate unconsciously and define in a basic 'taken for granted' fashion an organization's view of itself and its environment."

Culture is often described as the "organization's personality." Human personalities define who we are. They explain why we choose to do certain things and avoid other things. Our personality is shaped by our early experiences and ongoing socialization. Personalities take a long time to develop. Our personality is the behavioral manifestation of our values. The human personality and its development parallel organizational culture. That is, corporate culture is the behavioral manifestation of the corporation's core values. It takes a long time to develop and is fairly resistant to change.

Most people have only one personality. Likewise, corporate culture is the behavioral manifestation of the organization's core values by all, or certainly most, employees. And, just like the human personality, there should be just one corporate culture! The existence of many different subcultures in an organization makes organizational dysfunction more likely. In some healthcare organizations, for instance, there is an administrative culture, a physician culture, a nurse culture, a day shift culture, a night shift culture, and possibly more. When so many subcultures exist, it is impossible to create engagement, much less solidify sustainable engagement.

Culture is most associated with anthropology. In an article for the *International Journal for Quality in Healthcare*, Patricia M. Hudelson (2004, 345) defines culture as "a shared set of (implicit and explicit) values, ideas, concepts and rules of behavior that allow a social group to function and perpetuate itself. Rather than simply the presence or absence of a particular attribute, culture is understood as the dynamic and evolving socially constructed reality that exists in the minds of social group members."

An easy way to understand culture is to think of it as everything we do that is not genetically determined. For example, our eye color is not culturally determined, but the choices we make to wear glasses, have laser eye surgery, or wear contact lenses are influenced by the culture in which we live. The simplest way to define culture is to say that it is what we do when no one is looking. In the United States, most people speak English, wear Western-style clothes, eat Western-style foods, and follow traditional American sports. If we were to visit cities in Europe, the Middle East, Asia, Africa, or South America, we would see the populations there speaking, eating, and dressing differently. Ask someone outside the United States about football, and they will talk enthusiastically about what we call soccer! These differences are all culturally determined. The most important lesson about societal culture, as well as corporate culture, is that the behaviors that define the local culture are *learned*. Any behavior that is learned can, in theory, be unlearned or replaced with a different behavior. While culturally specific behavioral changes are possible, they are extremely difficult to achieve and take a long time.

Corporate culture has many of the same dynamics that define anthropological culture. Corporate culture is a set of value-based behaviors that are consistent across all staff in an organization. The corporate culture of any organization is, quite simply, "the way we do it here." Corporate culture is the most important determinant of sustainable employee engagement. Corporate culture also explains *why* we do things this way. Culture answers the questions "What do we do?" and "Why do we do it this way?"

DEFINING CULTURE

Culture is the tacit social order of an organization: It shapes attitudes and behaviors in wide-ranging and durable ways. Cultural norms define what is encouraged, discouraged, accepted, or rejected within a group. When culture is properly aligned with personal values, drives, and needs, it can unleash tremendous energy toward a shared purpose. When the workforce is highly engaged, a strong organizational culture will foster a capacity to thrive.

Culture can evolve flexibly and autonomously in response to changing opportunities and demands. Whereas strategy is typically determined by the C-suite, culture is more fluid, blending the intentions of top leaders with the knowledge and experiences of frontline employees.

Corporate culture is built on the foundation of the organization's mission, values, and vision. Exhibit 6.1 shows how these three elements come together to create the corporate culture.

Exhibit 6.1 Strength of Culture

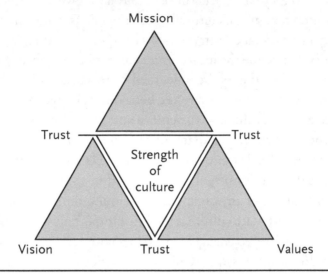

Remember that:

- The mission statement describes why the company exists. It expresses the organization's fundamental purpose—its corporate charter.
- Core corporate values are the drivers of behaviors and the basis for all decisions.
- The vision statement describes a future state. The vision is used to create the organization's strategic, departmental, and individual performance plans.

Exhibit 6.2 is an example of how the mission, values, and vision provide a framework for the corporate culture of the American College of Healthcare Executives (ACHE).

In a 2018 blog post for McKinsey & Company, Carolyn Dewer and Reed Doucette argue that "what often separates the

Exhibit 6.2 ACHE Mission, Vision, and Values

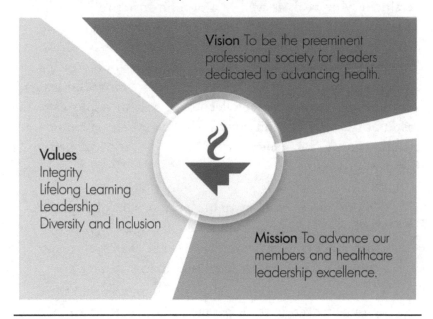

Vision To be the preeminent professional society for leaders dedicated to advancing health.

Values
Integrity
Lifelong Learning
Leadership
Diversity and Inclusion

Mission To advance our members and healthcare leadership excellence.

Source: ACHE (2021).

highest-performing organizations from the rest is culture." They identify six elements of corporate culture:

1. Define behavior changes that unlock business performance . . .
2. Uncover root cause mindsets and reframe them . . .
3. Engineer major business initiatives to role model and reinforce the desired culture . . .
4. Adjust work to create a coherent employee experience . . .
5. Produce opportunities for individuals to overcome personal barriers to change . . .
6. Lead the journey in rigorous and employee-centric ways.

The authors conclude that "we frequently see culture treated as a side project, without the rigor commensurate with a major business initiative. Our research shows that organizations with higher performing cultures create a 3× return to shareholders."

Henry Mintzberg is a highly regarded professor at McGill University in Montreal, as well as a prolific writer on the subjects of leadership and strategy. In a 2009 *Harvard Business Review* article, Mintzberg presents a view of organizational culture as a [community] that provides some useful lessons for increasing and sustaining employee engagement. He asks, "How [do leaders] get from the company as a collection of human resources to the institution as a community of human beings—from heroic leadership to engaged management?" Mintzberg (2009, 4) presents a five-part answer.

1. "Community building in organizations may best begin with small groups of committed managers." (This important concept about how leaders change corporate culture is discussed in detail later in this chapter.)
2. "A sense of community takes root as managers in these groups reflect on the experiences they have shared in the organization."
3. "The insights generated by these reflections naturally trigger small initiatives that grow into big strategies." (This is similar to Jim Collins's [2001, 334] "flywheel" concept of organizational change.)
4. "As these initial teams promote change, they become examples for other groups that spread 'communityship' throughout the organization."
5. "An organization knows that communityship is firmly established when members reach out in socially active, responsible, and mutually beneficial ways to the broader community."

A strong corporate culture is directly tied to an organization's financial performance. In 1992, John Kotter and James Heskett published their extensive research on 200 companies. The research purpose was to determine how corporate culture affected each company's

Exhibit 6.3 Kotter and Heskett: How Corporate Culture Affects Financial Performance

	Average Increase for 12 Firms with Performance-Enhancing Culture	Average Increase for 20 Firms without Performance-Enhancing Culture
Revenue growth	682%	166%
Employment growth	282%	36%
Stock price growth	901%	74%
Net income growth	756%	1%

Source: Data from Kotter and Heskett (1992, 95).

economic performance. Exhibit 6.3 shows the financial growth of companies with and without a performance-enhancing culture.

These amazing differences provide evidence that a strong corporate culture creates sustainable employee engagement, which, in turn, drives financial performance. But what happens when corporate culture is weak? Remember that a strong corporate culture is characterized by all employees behaving in ways that reflect the core values of the organization. Variation in values-based behaviors or complete disregard of the core corporate values poses significant risk to the organization. Two examples make this point: Wells Fargo Bank and Mount Carmel Health System.

In February 2018, Wells Fargo lost nearly $30 billion in market capitalization in one day. The Wells Fargo group that was responsible for opening new accounts clearly was not motivated by the company's core corporate values: "What's right for the consumer; People as a competitive advantage; Ethics; Diversity; Inclusion; and Leadership." Notice that "ethics" is one of Wells Fargo's core values. And yet, when then sales group sold two million accounts without customers' authorization, it was not motivated at all by ethics! It is reasonable to assume that the sales group was driven by the possibility of personal financial gain rather than the belief that ethics should guide their sales decisions.

A second example of a breach of corporate culture is Mount Carmel Health System in Columbus, Ohio. On its website, Mount Carmel identifies six core values: reverence, commitment to those who are poor, justice, stewardship, integrity, and safety. However, these values were ignored in the case of a Dr. William Husel, who, according to the Associated Press on June 5, 2019, was charged with the murder of 25 hospital patients.

Mount Carmel Health System has a long history of a strong corporate culture based on its core values. How is it possible, then, for a health system with such a great reputation and historically strong culture to experience a catastrophic breech of culture?

The reason why Dr. Husel purposely administered fatal doses of fentanyl may never be known. The bigger concern is that, even though a physician writes an order for a medication, many people are involved between the physician's order and the administration of the drug. How did the nurses, pharmacists, quality control personnel, and other physicians not notice the excessive amounts of fentanyl being given, as well as the unusually high number of deaths?

One can only speculate as to why so many highly trained professionals enabled this situation. It is clear that Mount Carmel's core values were not driving any of the decisions—especially reverence and safety. One could make a case that Dr. Husel created a powerful subculture in which the physician was seen as infallible, to be followed no matter what one's internal voice may be saying. Clearly, the values of the subculture that Husel created took precedence over the health system's core values.

Patrick Lencioni explains how something like the Mount Carmel problem could happen in a 2002 *Harvard Business Review* article. The article begins with an eye-opening statement. Lencioni (2002, 113) writes, "Take a look at this list of values: Communication, Respect. Integrity, Excellence. They sound pretty good, don't they? Strong, concise, meaningful. Maybe they even resemble your own company's values, the ones you spent so much time writing, debating and revising. If so, you should be very nervous. These are the corporate values of Enron. . . . And, as events have shown, they are not meaningful, they are meaningless."

Lencioni makes a key point for healthcare leaders who want their organization's values to anchor the culture and become the glue for employee engagement. Lencioni (2002, 114) concludes, "If you're not willing to accept the pain real values incur, don't bother going to the trouble of formulating a values statement."

The employee engagement model presented in this book begins with the premise that to have sustainable engagement, organizations must align employees' personal values with the core corporate values. Without such alignment, there is a great risk for the emergence of aberrant subcultures—which in the worst case could replicate the Mount Carmel Health System experience.

The research is clear: A strong corporate culture results in strong financial and other strategic business benefits. So, as I have repeated throughout this book, it is necessary to begin with aligned values. Once the values are aligned, then, as Lencioni suggests, one must be "willing to accept the pain real values incur." The leader's main responsibility in minimizing the pain that values incur is to create a comprehensive, consistent, and pervasive communication strategy. The best model for healthcare CEOs and other leaders in healthcare organizations is the "chief culture officer." When daily tasks and decisions are anchored in the organization's core values, and explained thoroughly by organizational leaders using values-based language, the likelihood of creating a strong corporate culture increases greatly. While it may sound cliché and a bit simplistic, leaders' communication content and style are the keys to a strong corporate culture that produces sustainable employee engagement.

LEADERSHIP COMMUNICATION TO STRENGTHEN CORPORATE CULTURE

What is effective communication? And why is communication so important? Too often, communication is just considered talking.

While talking is an important component of communication, it is greatly overrated. Communication is not so much what we say, it is what is heard and understood by the receiver. How many times has a leader made a presentation and later heard some of the interpretations of what was said. The leader responds, "They didn't listen! They didn't understand! They twisted my words!" For the purposes of building a strong corporate culture, a good working definition of communication is that it is not what is said, but what is heard by the receiver.

Why is the leader's day-to-day communication so important in creating and strengthening corporate culture? The most effective leaders have a clear purpose for communicating to staff that directs behaviors toward specific outcomes. Culture-building communication is more than "chatting" or "shooting the breeze." The most effective communication includes talking *and* listening. In a strong culture with highly engaged staff, everyone has an equal right to articulate their thoughts, actively listen, and ask clarifying questions. Finally, meaningful culture-focused communication has appropriate metrics and follow-ups on the goals that result from leader–follower communication.

Remember that the cornerstones of an organization's corporate culture are the mission (why the company exists), values (the organization's decision rules), and vision (the organization's future state). Communication that clarifies the mission is not complicated, but healthcare leaders must devote time and effort to talk with staff and reach agreement on the organization's collective purpose. This agreement about each department's purpose creates the framework for what people actually do as part of their everyday work.

Discussions about values have extraordinary power in strengthening the organization's corporate culture and employee engagement. Departments that talk about how they demonstrate their values with the people they serve tend to show remarkable cohesiveness and an increased dedication to their work. It is reasonable to assume that the Wells Fargo fraud case and the Mount Carmel Health System crisis would never have happened if frequent and meaningful values discussions had taken place.

Vision discussions are important because they communicate the end result that the organization is striving toward and how each employee's actions contribute to the achievement of the vision. Role clarification should always be contextualized in terms of how each person's tasks positively affect the success of the vision. And, performance metrics must be tied directly to the vision.

Profiles of Performance

Tina Freese Decker: Healthcare Is About People

Tina Freese Decker, FACHE, is the president and CEO of Spectrum Health, headquartered in Grand Rapids, Michigan. Tina leads a health system that generates $8 billion per year and employs more than 31,000 people. Her exceptional leadership has been often recognized nationally. Tina was named to *Modern Healthcare*'s "Top Women Leaders" list in 2019 and 2021; *Crain's Detroit Business*'s 2019 "Health Care Heroes" and 2018 "Most Notable Women in Health Care" lists; and *Managed Healthcare Executive*'s "10 Emerging Healthcare Industry Leaders" list in 2018.

Tina's personal leadership philosophy is based on her strong belief that healthcare is "about people." Her unwavering focus is on "the people we serve and those that serve them." I interviewed Tina in January 2021, during one of the most difficult months of the COVID-19 pandemic. She talked about how direct care providers have worked to the point of exhaustion to care for COVID-19 patients as well as all of the other healthcare needs in Spectrum Health's service area.

(continued)

(continued from previous page)

To help her staff with the effects of fatigue, frustration, and uncertainty, Tina created an Office of Physician and APP (Advanced Practice Provider) Fulfillment. The singular purpose of this office is to intervene, assist, and ameliorate the effects of caregiver burnout.

Tina's approach to employee engagement is based on the organization's mission, values, and vision. She believes that staff are always looking for a greater purpose. They want an answer to the question "why work here?" Tina believes that Spectrum Health's mission, values, and vision serve as a "guiding star" for staff, especially during difficult times, such as the COVID-19 pandemic. Data on Spectrum Health's employee satisfaction demonstrate the effectiveness of Tina's leadership. Spectrum Health was above the benchmark in terms of employee satisfaction going into the pandemic, and internal measures of employee satisfaction have stayed steady at 72 points—a significant accomplishment, given the immense challenges and stress associated with COVID-19.

In 2018, Tina chose to renew the organization's focus on cultural development. Through a comprehensive and inclusive six-month process, Spectrum Health's mission, values, and vision were revised to better represent the current healthcare environment (exhibit 6.4).

These cultural elements were approved in March 2019 and rolled out across the system over a six- to nine-month period. Tina states, "Now we are all operating using the same compass." In the development and creation of the new mission, values, and vision, Tina believes that the critical element is "communication times 10—with an emphasis on listening." Employee engagement is a never-ending process

(continued)

(continued from previous page)

of emphasizing the mission, values, and vision and listening to staff about how they use these cultural elements in their work. Tina states that in terms of long-term success, "It all depends on culture, which brings us together, energizes us and makes the very difficult work of caring for others exciting."

Exhibit 6.4 Components of Spectrum Health's Corporate Culture

Mission *Why Spectrum Health exists:*
To improve health, inspire hope and save lives

Vision
Values

What Spectrum Health is working to achieve:

Personalized health made simple, affordable and exceptional

The beliefs that underpin Spectrum Health's decisions:

• Compassion
• Collaboration
• Curiosity
• Courage

SUMMARY

Corporate culture is the most important predictor of sustainable employee engagement. An organization's corporate culture is its personality. In human beings, it is healthy to have only one personality. Likewise, in organizations, it is wise to have one dominant corporate culture. Having multiple subcultures can lead to disaster, as illustrated by the Wells Fargo and Mount Carmel Health System cases.

Corporate culture begins with the mission statement, which explains why the organization exists. Next, it is critical to identify the organization's core corporate values. This typically short list of values should be the basis for most of the decisions made by the board of trustees, executives, and staff. This list becomes a "code of conduct" for all employees. The final element of corporate culture is the vision. This is a statement of a future state that is highly desirable. The vision is the basis for the strategic plan, operational and departmental plans, individual performance objectives, and meaningful metrics. As staff see their efforts supporting the mission, their decisions grounded in the core values, and their work tasks moving the organization closer to the vision, employee engagement will grow.

QUESTIONS FOR ASSESSMENT AND DISCUSSION

Thinking about your own organization, respond to the following statements on a scale of 1 to 5, where 5 = strongly agree, 4 = agree, 3 = uncertain, 2 = disagree, and 1 = strongly disagree.

1. Our organization has clear and well-known statements on mission, core values, and vision.

2. We use our cultural elements to hire, retain, and promote staff.

3. Everyone in this organization can articulate who we are, what we stand for, and where we are headed.

4. Everyone in this organization knows the expected behaviors for their work based on the core values.

5. All change programs are put in the context of our mission, values, and vision.

REFERENCES

American College of Healthcare Executives (ACHE). 2021. "About ACHE." Accessed May 4. www.ache.org/about-ache.

Associated Press. 2019. "Ohio Doctor Charged with Murder of 25 Hospital Patients." *Wall Street Journal*, June 5.

Collins, J. C. 2001. *Good to Great: Why Some Companies Make the Leap and Others Don't*. New York: HarperCollins.

Dewer, C., and R. Doucette. 2018. "6 Elements to Create a High-Performing Culture." McKinsey and Company. Published April 20. www.mckinsey.com/business-functions/organization/our-insights/the-organization-blog/6-elements-to-create-a-high-performing-culture.

Hudelson, P. M. 2004. "Culture and Quality: An Anthropological Perspective." *International Journal for Quality in Healthcare* 16 (5): 345–46.

Kotter, J. P., and J. L. Heskett. 1992. *Culture and Performance*. New York: Free Press.

Lencioni, P. 2002. "Make Your Values Mean Something," *Harvard Business Review* 80 (7): 113–17, 126.

Mintzberg, H. 2009. "Rebuilding Companies as Communities." *Harvard Business Review* 87 (7): 104–43.

Schein, E. H. 2017. *Organizational Culture and Leadership*, 5th ed. Hoboken, NJ: John Wiley and Sons.

CHAPTER 7

The Leader's Role

The first responsibility of a leader is to define reality.
The last is to say thank you. In between, the leader is a servant.
—Max De Pree

Leadership is the capacity to translate vision into reality.
—Warren Bennis

Before you are a leader, success is about growing yourself.
When you become a leader, success is about growing others.
—Jack Welch

DEFINING LEADERSHIP

"Leaders have followers. Being called a chief executive officer and standing in front of a group docs not in itself make anyone a leader. Without committed followers, you have nothing but a title" (Atchison 2004, 1).

Titles are typically a function of the job position on an organization chart. There is no direct, automatic relationship between having a title and having followers. Titles are given, whereas followers are earned. Although this simple definition has some utility, it is also incomplete. An investigation of research articles on the definition of leadership can be exhausting. Each author seems to have their own spin on what is leadership, how it manifests, how it is developed, and to what degree is it situational. A common example of situational leadership is Winston Churchill: The British prime minister was widely applauded for leading England through the difficult times of World War II, but he was considered less relevant after the war. So, is all leadership situational? Or is there a set of fixed attributes that can be applied across multiple situations? Can these salient leadership characteristics be taught to everyone? And, there is the ubiquitous question, "Are leaders born, or are they made?"

In a thoughtful and well-researched article titled "What Is Leadership?," Alberto Silva (2016) of Keiser University noted that leadership scholar Warren Bennis "estimated, at the end of the last century, there were at least 650 definitions of leadership." Silva attempted to glean from them a useful leadership definition for today's challenges. According to Silva (2016, 3), leadership is a process of "interactive influence that occurs when, in a given context, some people accept someone as their leader to achieve common goals." He lists five factors that make up his definition of leadership:

1. Leadership is a process and not just a personal quality.
2. The leadership process is characterized by influence, not only the influence of the leader upon followers, as described by many authors, but the interactive influence between the leader and followers.
3. The leadership process occurs in a given context. If the context changes, the leadership process will also be different.
4. The leadership process requires that people, the followers, accept someone as their leader.
5. The purpose of the leadership process is to accomplish shared goals between leaders and followers.

This definition of leadership is useful because it helps explain the complexity of the relationship between leaders and followers. It also shows what leadership *is not*. For example, leadership is not management. Management and leadership have fundamentally different dynamics. Any list of leadership characteristics will typically include descriptions such as *motivator, communicator, courageous, visionary, strategic,* and *people-oriented.* A similar list of the characteristics of managers will usually include qualities such as *tactical, detail-oriented, organized, technical, focused,* and *data-driven.* Looking at these two lists, we can conclude that the main outcome of effective leadership is "inspired followers," and the main outcome of effective management is "predictable results." The contributions of both leaders and managers are critical to sustain organizational viability and employee engagement. The most successful organizations have inspired followers who are able to get predictable results. Here are some basic thoughts to reinforce the differences between and yet the interdependence of leadership and management:

- Leaders optimize the upside, and managers minimize the downside.
- Leaders envision possibilities, and managers calculate probabilities.
- Leaders focus on the what, and managers focus on the how.
- Leaders seize opportunities, and managers avert threats.
- Leaders provide vision, and managers provide execution.

Individuals often progress from their specific professional responsibilities to become a manager and then a leader. The two variables that define this progression from professional to manager to leader are *control* and *influence.* Exhibit 7.1 shows this progression.

Professionals have a great deal of control over how they perform the specific tasks required by their jobs. Managers have a fair amount of control over the planning, budgeting, and implementation of departmental objectives. However, managers do not control the specific tasks completed by each departmental employee. Managers need to use their influence to maximize employee motivation. In this way, management is a balance between control and influence.

Exhibit 7.1 Professional, Manager, Leader

Professional--Manager--Leader

Control ··· Influence

Technical   Management   Leadership

The CEO and other high-level leaders have virtually no control but exert a great deal of influence.

Jim Collins, in his outstanding book *Good to Great: Why Some Companies Make the Leap and Others Don't* (2001), created a five-level hierarchy that describes the evolution from a good employee to a high-performing leader (exhibit 7.2). Collins's hierarchy shows how employee engagement is a function of the level of leadership.

Exhibit 7.2 Five Levels of Leadership

Source: Collins (2001, 21).

This book has presented an engagement hierarchy that begins with the alignment of individual employees' values with the organization's core corporate values. The alignment of personal and corporate values allows employees to connect with the organization's vision and find meaning in their work. Combining the engagement model outlined in this book with Collins's hierarchy, it is clear that his Level 4 leader is the kind of leader who strengthens engagement through meaningful work. A Level 4 leader "catalyzes commitment to and vigorous pursuit of a clear and compelling vision, stimulating higher performance standards." Based on the engagement model presented in this book, we could add to Collins's Level 4 definition: "Allows employees to increase their engagement because they see their specific tasks contributing to vision achievement. They find their work meaningful" (Collins 2001, 20).

The main premise of this book is that sustainable engagement results when employees find purpose in their work. Purpose is found in connecting to the mission of the organization. Meaningful work occurs when employees connect their performance to the vision. But the nature of the vision is that it is time-specific. Therefore, employee engagement that is rooted in the vision will diminish or disappear after the vision is achieved. There is no such dynamic with the organization's mission. The mission of the organization is, in theory, unchanging. If an organization changes its mission, it changes the fundamental reason the company exists. So, when employee engagement is inextricably tied to the mission, a high degree of sustainable engagement is the result.

Collins's Level 5 leaders are necessary to create an environment—a corporate culture—that allows employees to find purpose in their work through their connection to the organization's mission. According to Collins (2001, 20), a Level 5 leader "builds enduring greatness through a paradoxical blend of personal humility and professional will." The key words in this definition are "enduring greatness." Collins lists a number of companies that meet his criteria for "enduring greatness." However, his examples include no healthcare delivery systems. The Profiles of Performance throughout this book showcase several Level 5 leaders.

An older but relevant article is Christopher A. Bartlett and Sumantra Ghoshal's "Changing the Role of Top Management: Beyond Strategy to Purpose" (1994) in the *Harvard Business Review*. Although this article is decades old, its lessons are still important for today's healthcare leaders. Uncertainty and change in the healthcare industry have only increased, exacerbated by the retirement of the baby boom generation and influx of millennials and members of Generation Z. Most important is the impact of all the difficulties associated with the COVID-19 pandemic and the post-pandemic realities. Bartlett and Ghoshal (1994, 80) discuss the evolution of organizations: "Over time, as corporate size and diversity expanded, strategies, structures, and reporting and planning systems, became more complex. Employees' daily activities became increasingly fragmented and systematized." This statement, written in 1994, easily describes today's healthcare industry, with its emphasis on expanding the size of healthcare systems and systematizing ever-fragmenting employee activities.

Bartlett and Ghoshal (1994, 80) study a number of successful companies that approach business growth differently:

[These companies' leaders] share a surprisingly consistent philosophy. First, they place less emphasis on following a clear strategic plan than on building a rich, *engaging corporate purpose*. Next, they focus less on formal structural design and more on effective management processes. Finally, they are less concerned with controlling employees' behavior than with developing their capabilities and broadening their perspectives. In sum, they have moved beyond the old doctrine of strategy, structure, and systems to a softer, more organic model built on the development of purpose, process and people.

According to Bartlett and Ghoshal, the most successful leaders behave in ways that make purpose their "North Star." They suggest that leaders do the following: First, they recommend that leaders move from "setting strategy to defining purpose." The authors believe that "in most corporations today, people no longer know—or even care—what or why their companies are. In such an environment, leaders have an urgent role to play. Obviously. They must retain control over the processes that frame the company's strategic priorities. But strategies can engender strong, enduring emotional attachments only when they are imbedded in a broader organizational purpose" (Bartlett and Ghoshal 1994, 81).

Second, Bartlett and Ghoshal discuss their concept of "embedding corporate ambition." They write that, "Traditionally, top-level managers have tried to engage employees intellectually through the pervasive logic of strategic analyses. But clinically framed and contractually based relationships do not inspire the extraordinary effort and sustain commitment required to deliver consistently superior performance. For that, companies need employees who care, who have a strong emotional link with the organization" (Bartlett and Ghoshal 1994, 81).

Third, they suggest that leaders create a process of "instilling organizational values." They conclude that "instilling values takes more than inspiring speeches. At least the speeches can confirm the message sent by senior executives' daily actions. Management is the message, speeches only can call attention to it" (Bartlett and Ghoshal 1994, 85).

Finally, the authors believe that the most successful leaders find ways to give meaning to employees' work. "In the main, every individual extracts the most basic sense of purpose from personal fulfillment he or she derives from being part of an organization. More than just providing work, companies can help give meaning to people's lives" (Bartlett and Ghoshal 1994, 86).

THE LEADER'S MAIN ROLE—TO LEAD CHANGE

Lead change, manage change, or react to change—these are the realities of today's healthcare delivery systems. Before the COVID-19 pandemic, change in healthcare delivery was relatively linear and, for the most part, driven by changes in regulations and financing. The pandemic demanded radical, rapid, and sometime risky changes in the way healthcare was delivered. Most hospitals reduced, stopped, or delayed elective surgeries. That meant that many patients with serious conditions were unable to get the care they needed. COVID-19 patients filled intensive care units (ICUs). Many large tertiary care centers had very few or no ICU beds. Workloads increased dramatically, resulting in massive fatigue. The information from the federal and state governments seemed inconsistent at best, causing a great deal of frustration. The challenge for healthcare leaders in the COVID-19 environment was, and continues to be, unprecedented. However, those leaders who excelled during the crisis were the same ones who were strong leaders before the pandemic. The lesson is that while some people may be situational leaders, more often, the best leaders will shine in any situation. These exceptional leaders use the art and science of leadership regardless of what the environment throws at them. They are the ones who will make the most of the lessons of the pandemic to improve their organization's delivery systems.

ORGANIZATIONAL CHANGE—THE BASICS

The main role of a leader is to design and lead organizational improvement—that is, change. A great number of books and articles have been written about how leaders inspire change, but too few of these publications define the concept of organizational change. Organizational change is the process of moving from A to B, where B is better than A. Within this simple definition lie many complexities. For example, what is A—the current status? How is it defined or described? Does everyone agree what A looks like? And, more importantly, if everyone agrees on the description of A—the current status—does everyone think it needs to change?

Once there is agreement on these questions, then the hard part begins. We know what A is and that it needs to change. What does it need to change to? What is the most desirable alternative (B) to the current situation? Far too often, senior executives promote organizational change because they want to pursue the latest healthcare delivery fad or because they feel that if they don't stimulate change, bad things might happen. Of course, the worst reason to initiate change is in reaction to market shift or another environmental crisis. Remember, trustees and senior executives can either lead, manage, or react to change. If they are not leading or managing change, then they are likely reacting to change. How does the leader's role in the change process affect the level and sustainability of employee engagement?

ORGANIZATIONAL CHANGE—TWO MYTHS AND REALITIES

Myth #1: Humans resist change. How many times have you heard, "I want to change this organization for the better, but people always resist change!" There is no greater myth about human behavior. Life is about change. In organizations, there is a tendency to blame the "resistance to change" on a basic human condition. This is a false premise and deleterious to moving the organization forward. The perceived resistance is not a fundamental human trait, but rather a function of the leader's communication approach and style. See Realities #1 and #2 for the best ways to lead a change process.

Reality #1: Humans love to change! We change all the time. Consider, for instance, the story of a nurse who got married. First, he married a person from a different state. Then, he decided to hyphenate his name after marriage, adding his spouse's name to his own. Let's count the changes: He changed his name. He changed his state of residence. He changed jobs. He needed to change his state nursing license. And, of course, he changed the person he lived with. Did this nurse show resistance to these "life-changing" decisions, or did he enthusiastically embrace each of these difficult changes? The answer is that at no time in this process was there any "human resistance to change." Why, then, do so many people buy into the

Exhibit 7.3 The Dynamics of Change: Easy to Hard

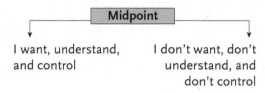

The Easy-to-Hard Continuum

| | Midpoint | |

I want, understand, and control

I don't want, don't understand, and don't control

myth that humans resist change, when there are daily examples of individuals enthusiastically changing significant parts of their lives? The answer, illustrated in exhibit 7.3, is simple.

This exhibit shows that humans resist change when they don't want it, don't understand it, or don't control the aspects of the change that affect their work. However, all humans will change when they want, understand, and control the change. Highly engaged employees will support changes when they are sufficiently involved to want, understand, and control the desired change. How this level of engagement can be created is discussed in chapter 8.

Myth #2: "I want happy employees, and I want to lead change." I have heard stories about human resources executives who were assigned the task of increasing employee satisfaction and engagement, usually after a biannual employee survey. Maybe the survey results were less than expected or desired by the CEO and trustees. Typically, the next step would be for the CEO to assign the task of increasing the number to the human resources executive. This step is usually taken during a change process. This is the core of the myth— employee satisfaction cannot be increased during a change process!

Reality #2: It is undesirable for employees to have high satisfaction during a change process. In an effective change process, employee satisfaction will always go down! Exhibit 7.4 shows the relationship between employee satisfaction and organizational change.

High employee satisfaction during a change process significantly dilutes the potential for the change process to succeed. Why? When

Exhibit 7.4 The Dynamics of Change: The Anxiety/Behavior Continuum

The Anxiety/Behavior Continuum

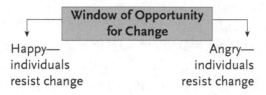

Happy—
individuals
resist change

Angry—
individuals
resist change

employees are happy, they are happy with the status quo, or some imagined ideal of their current status. In this circumstance, employees will resist change because they are happy with their current job situation. On the other hand, if the change process is too frustrating, to the point that employees are angry, they will also resist organizational change processes. The "art of organizational change" is to find the window of opportunity for change. Or, as some learning theories suggest, the individual must be in a state of cognitive disequilibrium. Employees must be a little unhappy with the current situation, but not to the point of anger.

Profiles of Performance

Alan Kaplan: We Must Keep Our Caregivers Healthy

Alan Kaplan, MD, FACHE, has been the CEO of UW Health, an academic medical center in Madison, Wisconsin, since May 2016. Alan has spent 25 years in senior leadership positions. UW Health comprises seven hospitals and several non-hospital healthcare facilities, employs 15,000 staff and 1,500 physicians, and generates $3.6 billion in annual revenue. UW Health's flagship hospital was ranked 17th on *US News & World Report*'s list of the top US hospitals. These impressive

(continued)

(continued from previous page)

quantitative facts are attributable to Alan's leadership style. He is a role model for everything discussed in this chapter about leadership.

Alan's LinkedIn page says it best: "For 25 years as a senior healthcare executive, Dr. Alan Kaplan has dedicated his career to improving the health of patients and communities. Known for his ability to navigate conflict and difficult historical barriers, Dr. Kaplan helped create a unified patient-focused, joint operating agreement between Wisconsin's largest academic medical center and a highly regarded community hospital. This partnership includes regional financial risk sharing, consolidation of employed specialist providers and merger of their respective provider-owned health plans, which now serves 350,000 members. A lifelong learner and part-time conservation farmer, Dr. Kaplan is the author of a series of articles that share his reflections on his journey from full-time clinician to senior healthcare executive."

Alan agreed to be interviewed for this book about employee engagement because, as he stated, "The COVID-19 pandemic has brought engagement to the fore." He believes the focus on engagement is the result of the fact that "the pandemic pressures were laid upon an already increasingly complex delivery system where we have layered new technology, knowledge and costs." He went on: "Complex technology creates a universe of exponential growth of difficulty for everything." Alan realizes that this exponential growth of complexities and difficulties "goes on the backs of the employees." During the pandemic, and today, Alan believes that "we need to keep our caregivers healthy."

Alan's concern during the pandemic, amid ongoing changes in regulations and finances, was the effect of uncertainty on

(continued)

(continued from previous page)

UW Health's employees. His leadership style is to lead the process of ameliorating that uncertainty. A big part of his job is "to create as much certainty as possible." This is a daily personal expectation to "get rid of ambiguity." He promises to answer any question, no matter what the issue, emotional component, or circumstance. He rounds often and also expects the senior executive team to work hard to reduce ambiguity and create certainty in this uncertain world.

Alan has a strong sense of purpose, and he is focused on achievement. He says that he "wants to build things, to make things better." To achieve his goal, Alan has three guiding principles, which are underpinned by his personal credo: "Always seek to achieve, guided by a strong sense of integrity, which is more than honesty." His three healthcare leadership principles are:

1. An organization must have a three- to five-year strategic plan that is well known and helps maintain focus. Avoid too many changes that are not in the plan.

2. Be a responsive executive and management team. Demonstrate consistent behaviors that will strengthen trust and create followers.

3. We must learn to listen. We need to understand everyone's point of view. We need to listen, gather information, develop strategy, assign metrics, and, most of all, make prudent decisions.

This formula has worked for Alan in leading an organization that maximizes sustainable engagement, even during the most difficult times.

SUMMARY

This chapter examined the elusive and complex concept of leadership as it relates to creating sustainable employee engagement during difficult times. A leader, as Peter Drucker (1996) notes, is someone with followers. There is no argument that having a title such as CEO, president, senior executive, or chair is associated with leader status. However, without followers, these individuals are not leaders. This fact—that leaders have followers and that leadership is unrelated to titles—means that leadership can be found at all levels of the organization. In fact, it is possible that the CEO may have a big title and paycheck but no followers; therefore, this CEO is not a leader. But within the organization headed by a follower-less executive, there may be tens, if not hundreds, of leaders in clinical and nonclinical areas.

Leadership can be differentiated from management. While a large gray area lies between the functions of an organizational leader and those of an organizational manager, important differences exist. The main role of a leader is to inspire followers. The main role of a manager is to get predictable results. The most effective healthcare delivery systems emphasize both inspiration and predictability. The two main leadership resources are influence and relationship building. The two main management resources are specific tasks and metrics. Leaders seldom use control mechanisms—the essence of leadership is influence. Managers may use some influence, but their essence is captured by predictable, data-driven outcomes. The question of which is better, leadership or management, depends on what you are trying to achieve. Do you want an inspired workforce, or do you want predictable outcomes? The highest-performing healthcare organizations want both.

The main role of a leader, regardless of title, is to lead change. Organizational change was defined in this chapter as moving from A to B, where B is better than A. There are two main myths about change: that humans resist change, and that organizations want happy employees during a major change process. Remember, humans change all the time. Humans are amenable to change when we want the change, we understand the change, and we control the personal aspects of the change. And, remember that happy employees will resist change when they are happy with the current situation. The leadership challenge is to create a bit of disequilibrium so that they are not happy and see the change as an opportunity. One caveat: Don't create such cognitive dissonance that there is organizational chaos and employees become angry. Angry people will not embrace change.

A good summary of leadership is provided by Stephen R. Covey (1996) in the book *The Leader of the Future*. Covey's book chapter is as appropriate in a post-COVID-19 world as it was in 1996. Covey states,

> The leader of the future, of the next millennium, will be one who creates a culture or a value system centered on principles. Creating such a culture in a business, government, school, hospital, nonprofit organization, family, or other organization will be a tremendous and exciting challenge in this new era and will only be achieved by leaders, be they emerging or seasoned, who have the vision, courage, and humility to constantly learn and grow. Those people and organizations who have the passion for learning—learning through listening, seeing emerging trends, sensing and anticipating needs in the marketplace, evaluating past successes and mistakes, and absorbing the lessons that conscience and principles teach us, to mention just a few ways—will have enduring influence. Such learning leaders will not resist change; they will embrace it.

QUESTIONS FOR ASSESSMENT AND DISCUSSION

Thinking about yourself as a leader, respond to the following statements on a scale of 1 to 5, where 5 = strongly agree, 4 = agree, 3 = uncertain, 2 = disagree, and 1 = strongly disagree.

1. I invest more time in the future than in the past.
2. I am trusted throughout the organization.

3. Learning, coaching, and professional development are a big part of my daily work.
4. I invest two-thirds of my time in relationship building.
5. I routinely use active listening techniques.

REFERENCES

Atchison, T. A. 2004. *Followership: A Practical Guide to Aligning Leaders and Followers.* Chicago: Health Administration Press.

Bartlett, C. H., and S. Ghoshal. 1994. "Changing the Role of Top Management—Beyond Strategy to Purpose." *Harvard Business Review* 72 (6): 79–88.

Collins, J. C. 2001. *Good to Great: Why Some Companies Make the Leap and Others Don't.* New York: HarperCollins.

Covey, S. 1996. "Three Roles of the Leader in the New Paradigm." In *The Leader of the Future*, edited by F. Hesselbein, M. Goldsmith, and R. Beckhard, 149–59. New York: Jossey-Bass.

Drucker, P. F. 1996. *The Leader of the Future.* Edited by F. Hesselbein, M. Goldsmith, and R. Beckhard. San Francisco: Jossey-Bass.

Silva, A. 2016. "What Is Leadership?" *Journal of Business Studies Quarterly* 8 (1): 1–5.

CHAPTER 8

Recommended Professional and Organizational Processes

Success is not final, failure is not fatal: It is the courage to continue that counts.
—Winston Churchill

If you really look closely, most overnight successes took a long time.
—Steve Jobs

Even if you are on the right track, you'll get run over if you just sit there.
—Will Rogers

THE LEADER'S TOOLKIT

"If the only tool you have is a hammer, everything looks like a nail" is a common saying that explains the overuse of a particular process or technique. This is an ongoing challenge for healthcare leaders: to have a lot of tools in their toolbox—and, more importantly, to know which tool is the right one to use in each situation. This chapter will help healthcare leaders develop a broad and deep set of tools and offer guidance on which tools are best to use at each stage of increasing employee engagement. This book is about employee engagement, so the tools recommended in this chapter will focus

Exhibit 8.1 Model of Sustainable Employee Engagement

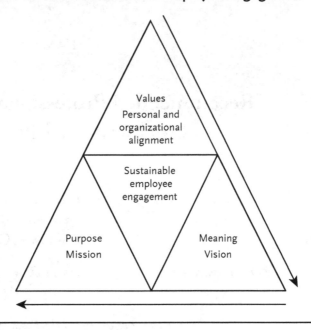

on the human condition within today's healthcare delivery systems. These human tools are the intangible elements—or the "soft stuff," as discussed in chapter 3—of organizational performance.

As a point of reference, let's review the model of sustainable employee engagement introduced in chapter 1 and shown again here in exhibit 8.1. This model provides the context for the professional and organizational process recommended in this chapter.

FACTOR 1: VALUES—WHY THEY ARE THE CRITICAL SUCCESS FACTOR

The most effective way to create sustainable employee engagement is to ensure that personal values are aligned with the core values that drive organizational decisions. Values alignment begins with recruitment and proceeds through candidate interviews, and it should be the single most important part of the final selection of new employees. And, organizational values must be the centerpiece of the onboarding process and all professional development and re-recruitment efforts.

Values alignment is the first, and non-negotiable, element in any employee engagement process. An organization that allows widely different values to drive decisions will always experience some degree of tension and conflict.

Step 1: Recruitment

Creating a values-aligned organization begins with recruitment. And recruitment begins with the advertisement for a position. As a small experiment, look at some local ads for nurses or other direct care providers. What words are used to describe the job? How many say things like, "Hospital is seeking a caring, compassionate, quality-focused professional for our patient-focused healthcare delivery system." More likely, the ads read like this: "Healthcare position opening, good pay and benefits, signing bonus, free parking, no mandatory overtime." It is clear from these two examples that the first hospital is hiring someone whose values are aligned with the organization, and the second is hiring someone who will be focused on money and benefits. Now read your organization's latest job posting for a nurse. Is it more like the first example or the second?

Recommendation: Ensure that your position descriptions reflect the core values of your organization.

Step 2: Interview and Selection

After your organization has recruited some potential new employees, the values alignment process moves to the interview stage. There is a large body of work on "values-based interviewing" and "targeted selection." Human resources professionals should be skilled in these techniques, and all healthcare professionals who employ others should know the basics. When interviewing the final candidates for a position, some universal values should be addressed. For example, regardless of the position, it is important that future employees be able to articulate their degree of integrity, professionalism, accountability, and readiness to be a team member. Beyond these fundamental work values, it is critical for the interviewer to be absolutely clear about the organization's core values and the unique aspects of the culture that the prospective employee would be joining.

One question is useful to discern a potential employee's values: "What can you tell me about yourself that would help us make our employment decision?" Listen carefully for the use of the singular pronouns "I/me" versus the collective pronouns "we/us." For example, if the candidate's answer is loaded with "I did this," "I know how to do this," and "I can help you with this," then the candidate has an individualistic mindset. Compare these answers with "Our team did this in my last job," "We were able to accomplish this," and "The company saw us as an asset." The use of singular versus plural pronouns is a key indicator of an independent personality or a team player. Pronouns are important in values-based interviewing. This is just one example of interviewing for values. A good follow-up resource is Adele B. Lynn's 2008 book *The EQ Interview*. Earlier in this book, we discussed the importance of emotional intelligence, especially in higher management and leadership positions. Lynn's book is easy to read, and its 250 behavior-based questions are useful for determining which candidates have the highest emotional intelligence.

Recommendation: Hire to fit, not to fill—that is, hire to fit to the corporate culture, not to fill a skill set.

Step 3: Onboarding

Your organization's help wanted advertisements attracted some good, values-driven candidates, and the interview process identified the best candidate to fit the corporate culture. Now the new employee needs to be acculturated. This begins with the onboarding process. Onboarding differs from the traditional "new employee orientation" in that it incorporates the information traditionally dispensed in orientation but goes beyond this basic information. New employee orientation is usually a one-time, relatively short meeting that introduces employees to the organization, discusses some basic human resources issues, and may include a presentation by the CEO or another senior executive. The main characteristic of the orientation is that it is a single meeting. Onboarding may begin with a traditional employee orientation, but it goes well beyond one meeting. New employees may be assigned a mentor whom they can call with questions. Some organizations plan one onboarding session per month for three months, as it may take 90 days to really get to know the organization.

In the orientations of most healthcare organizations, new employees typically learn about the organization's history, mission, human resources policies, and topics such as pay and benefits, insurance, and parking. In contrast, a good onboarding program typically lasts several months. At the initial meeting, new employees may be given the standard orientation but are also introduced to the CEO and some of the senor executives. The importance of the CEO's presentation is both tangible and symbolic. The tangible elements are a function of the content of the CEO's presentation, in which the organization's mission, values, and vision are personalized for new employees. In this process, the CEO needs to be seen as the "CCO"—the "chief culture officer." The presence of the CEO and senior executives also serves a symbolic function, making a powerful statement that employees are important.

Recommendation: Implement an onboarding process that lasts several months to help new employees acculturate to your organization.

Step 4: Professional Development

The COVID-19 pandemic and the post-pandemic environment, combined with rapid scientific and technological changes, require high-performance healthcare organizations to focus on lifelong learning. Ideally, each employee would create, in collaboration with their supervisor, an individual professional development plan. Such a plan would include time-specific learning goals and an associated budget item. Employees' learning objectives should be tied to specific work assignments and tasks that contribute to the achievement of the organization's vision.

Two important things happen as a result of employee professional development: The organization benefits from highly trained staff, and employees feel valued because the company is investing in them and helping them perform at a higher level—and possibly be ready for a promotion. The impact of professional development may be different depending on the employee's age. Generational differences in the workplace, though important, are beyond the scope of this book; however, data suggest that professional development has a greater impact among millennials.

Recommendation: Ensure that the budgetary line item for professional development increases every year—or at least that it never goes down. Professional development is not an expense, it is an investment!

Step 5: Re-recruitment

Organizations spend large amounts of cash and time on recruitment. Once an employee is hired, the recruitment process stops. But there is a better way—one that reduces turnover and increases employee engagement. The *re-recruitment process* begins by ranking employees according to their performance. A common ranking goes like this: A for exceptional performers, B for good performers with potential, and C for employees who do their jobs consistently but are not exceptional performers. The re-recruitment process focuses on the A performers. The team with the best players usually wins, and conversely, it is hard to win with a mediocre team. Every executive, director, and manager should have a list of their A, B, and C performers.

Re-recruiting the A players starts with one-on-one interviews that focus on the most important parts of their job. It is common practice for organizations to conduct exit interviews when staff leave. The data from such interviews may be very biased, depending on the employee's reason for leaving. Because the data can be contaminated, its utility is questionable. However, this is not the case with re-recruitment interviews. High performers tend to be honest about the best and worst parts of their job. These data, when gathered from a number of engaged A performers, will show a pattern that senior executives can use to create a higher-performing corporate culture. Here are some questions to ask in a re-recruitment interview:

- What do you take the most pride in as an employee?
- What part of your job is most rewarding?
- What does this organization do that you would not want to change?
- What changes could this organization make to make your job more rewarding?

Recommendation: Schedule one hour per day to interview high performers in your organization to learn what keeps them engaged in their work and committed to the organization.

FACTOR 2: MEANINGFUL WORK AS A FUNCTION OF ORGANIZATIONAL VISION

Remember: The organization's vision statement helps employees see how their specific tasks are tied directly to the creation of a better future.

Be sure that your organization's vision statement is inspirational, directional, and measurable. Does your vision statement create excitement and a sense of urgency? Does it set a clear road map for employees to follow? And, finally, can progress be measured daily, weekly, and monthly?

A metaphor may be useful to explain these vision elements. We use the vision process quite often in our personal lives. For example, planning a vacation begins with identifying the destination—Hawaii. Our vision is to go to Hawaii. It is inspirational, directional, and measurable (we know when we have arrived). This vision drives our strategy—when to go, how much time to take off work, and how to pay for the tickets and expenses. The strategy drives the tactical plans and individual performance goals—pack the luggage, take the dog to the vet, set the alarm to wake up on time, call a taxi to go to the airport, clear security, and board the plane. When the plane lands in Honolulu, our vision has been achieved.

Another common example of a vision in action is a retirement plan. Most workers have some sort of retirement plan: IRA, SEP, Roth, or Keogh. A retirement plan is a vision. It starts at the end—how much money do I need to retire, and at what age? Usually, this is a big number. But, if you start at a young age and create a multiyear strategy to reach a financial target (the retirement vision), then the tactical and individual performance requirements become clear—"I need to set aside this much each pay period, and get a little lucky with the stock market, and then I will be able to comfortably retire at 63." Vision, strategy, tactics, and individual performance goals are all governed by meaningful metrics. This process, which we use so easily in our personal lives, can be transferred to any healthcare organization. When done openly, with transparent data, employees can see that what they do has an impact on the organization's future success. At this point, employees find *meaning in their work*.

Recommendation: Create communication and feedback systems and processes that inform the employees about how their specific tasks help the organization achieve its vision of a better future.

FACTOR 3: FINDING PURPOSE IN THE MISSION

The mission statement is the reason the organization exists. Vision statements can (and should) change every few years to accommodate environmental realities. However, the mission statement and core values do not change. Once the mission and values change, then there is a new organization! This does happen in mergers and acquisitions, or sometimes an acute healthcare facility is reestablished as a specialty hospital. However, these situations are uncommon. The mission statement equals purpose, and, as we discussed earlier in this book, working toward a greater purpose is the highest form of employee engagement. Engagement is the outcome of finding a transcendent purpose in work.

Mihaly Csikszentmihalyi has completed years of research and written several books on his concept of "flow." Csikszentmihalyi (1993, xiii) writes,

> Though my research into creativity proved successful, something even more important emerged from my observations of artists at work. I called it flow, because this was the metaphor several respondents gave for how it felt when their experience was most enjoyable—it was like being carried away by a current, everything moving smoothly without effort. The first symptom of flow is a narrowing of attention on a clearly defined goal. We know what must be done, and we get immediate feedback as to how well we are doing.

Csikszentmihalyi's concept of flow is a scientific definition of what occurs during purpose-driven engagement. In his book *Good Business*, Csikszentmihalyi (2003, 42–55) describes eight elements that promote flow, or purpose-driven engagement: "1. Goals Are Clear; 2. Feedback Is Immediate; 3. A Balance Between Opportunity and Capacity; 4. Concentration Deepens; 5. The Present Is What Matters; 6. Control Is Not a Problem; 7. The Sense of Time is Altered; 8. Loss of Ego."

Recommendation: Allow opportunities for staff to "transcend" the notion of work as a series of completed tasks by connecting everything they do to the organization's mission. When their purpose matches their capacity to perform, and they have control over their actions, then flow, transcendence, and maximum engagement are possible.

FACTOR 4: SUSTAINABLE EMPLOYEE ENGAGEMENT

When employees' values are aligned with the core organizational values, when employees find meaningful work as a result of their contributions to the achievement of the vision, and when they find purpose in being a critical part of the mission, then all of the ingredients for sustainable engagement are in place. What is the catalyst needed to ignite such a level of engagement? What is the "secret sauce" that brings it all together? What is the "North Star" that guides the process of sustainable engagement? The answer to all these questions is *communication*.

The topic of communication is exceptionally detailed and complex. Hundreds of undergraduate and graduate programs are dedicated to the sciences of communication, linguistics, and psycho-linguistics. Many hundreds, and possibility thousands, of books and articles have been written about effective communication. So, it is with a measure of humility that this book attempts to identify and explain some of the communication concepts and techniques that successful healthcare leaders use to enhance employee engagement.

Three basic principles cover all elements of communication. The first principle is that communication is a system. This means that it takes two or more people for communication to occur. Implied in this principle is that the receiver shares responsibility for the transmission of the message.

The second principle is that it is impossible *not* to communicate. Whenever two or more people are interacting, messages are being sent and received. Interestingly, many of the messages we send are unintentional. Our facial expressions, gestures, and other behaviors are constantly being interpreted by others.

The third communication principle is that it is impossible to predict or control the interpretation of a message. No two people have the same personality, history, or perspective. For this reason, the lens through which an individual views the world will determine the interpretation of verbal and nonverbal communication. In terms of communication, perception equals reality. Given these principles, three guidelines should govern a leader's communication strategy to increase employee engagement.

Communication Guideline 1: Effective Communication Is Not What You Say, but What Is Heard

After a long staff meeting directed by the CEO of a large health system, several attendees commented that they had never been to a meeting where "the speaker talked so much and said so little." Others responded, "All I heard is that I should update my résumé and start looking for another job." Why did the staff feel this way after the meeting? The CEO was clear about the organization's strategy, the role of the senior leadership in producing strong financial performance, and the need to be ready for more change in the coming year. The presentation was well written and delivered, with visually attractive slides, and the CEO left ten minutes for questions at the end. Because there were no questions, the CEO assumed that the presentation had covered all of the relevant facts.

The CEO felt good after the presentation and was shocked when the organization's informal network reported several negative comments. The "natural" response of the CEO was to blame the employees: "They didn't listen—otherwise, they wouldn't feel this way. I wish they were more motivated and committed to the organization." Highly effective leaders know that they cannot blame the recipient of the communication for their interpretation of what was said.

Recommendation: When presenting information, always talk in the language of the receiver. For example, This book is written in English, the first language of the author. While this text may have some useful information, readers who do not speak English will be unable to understand it or find anything of value in it. Just like our primary spoken language, all humans are programmed with a predictable three-stage *language comprehension process*. The first stage is, How does this information affect me? This is the "egocentric" stage. The second stage is, How does this information affect my job? This is the "role-centric" stage. The third stage is, How does this affect my connection to the organization? This is the "strategy-centric" stage. The most effective leadership communication delivery process will follow this sequential pattern. The presenter must follow these three steps and state:

1. Here is what we are going to do. It is critical for everyone to know what will happen.
2. Here is why we are doing this. Always explain the context for the action. It is best if the context incorporates the cultural elements of mission, values, and vision.
3. And, most importantly, this is how the action will affect you, your job, and your relationship with the organization.

Communication Guideline 2: Listening Is Communication

Listening is arguably the most critical skill for creating followers. The best leaders know how and when to listen. Listening is a challenge in a highly complex, busy healthcare environment. "I don't have time to listen, there is too much to do." This is a statement that I hear often. But taking time to listen, and listen actively, is the best way to engage others in a task or process. For the purposes of this text, there are three important ways to listen: (1) selective or judgmental listening, (2) active listening, and (3) reflective listening.

Selective or judgmental listening is, all too often, the default response to a question. A simple example is when a staff member asks, "Why are we doing this task this way?" The supervisor responds by saying, "Because we get paid to do it, stop asking questions." This response is both *selective and judgmental,* and it is highly toxic to employee engagement. A leader who is skilled in *active listening* would respond with a series of questions: "From your point of view, is there a better way to do this task? Are there other tasks that would be more useful? What can we do together to achieve the best result?" The third kind of listening is called *reflective listening.* Reflective listening is used when a situation becomes emotional. The task for the leader in these situations is to turn down the emotion and return to active listening techniques. For example, a staff member may be frustrated to the point of crying. The leaders deals with the emotional context before dealing with the problematic content. Empathic questions are best used in reflective listening.

Recommendation: Much of healthcare is a process of diagnosis and treatment. Individuals pride themselves on coming to fast and definitive decisions. However, in terms of effective communication that strengthens engagement, listening to another person is better than solving their problem quickly. Leaders who practice active listening ask clarifying questions to identify the problem. Of course, spoken language is the main channel of communication. But *how* people say those words can be as important as the words themselves. The most effective leaders learn to communicate at several levels: talking, questioning, listening, discussing, and concluding. Throughout this sequence, the leader is sensitive to the nonverbal and emotional nuances embedded in the interaction.

Communication Guideline 3: Team Communication

Team building is a critical leadership skill and one that is important to employee engagement. (Team building will be discussed in more detail in chapter 10.) Communication dynamics are determined by the maturity of the team. New teams communicate differently than seasoned, long-standing teams. New teams require a great deal of verbal direction and feedback, whereas mature teams seem to function on a nonverbal, anticipatory level.

A useful example is a surgical team. Members of a surgical team who have worked together for many months or even years know exactly what the surgeon needs and when it is needed. The surgeon does not have to say, "give me this instrument now" because the team anticipates what is required. In contrast, a new surgical team needs to be told what to do at each step and requires feedback to assess whether the action was correct. Simply stated, new teams need "hyper-verbal" communication, and mature teams use "super-verbal" communication.

Recommendation: Team communication is a function of the time the members have been working together. Long-standing, high-performing teams can easily execute complicated tasks with a minimum of verbal interaction because each team member's performance expectations are well understood by the other team members. However, new teams that have not been working together for very long require focused communication about role expectations, combined with ample positive or corrective feedback. There is an important caveat, however: Any time you change a member of the team, you have a brand new team. For example, if a surgical team has been together for years and one person retires, this individual needs to be replaced. The replacement makes the once mature team brand-new again. The new team member will need a lot of verbal direction and feedback until behavioral expectations become anticipatory.

Profiles in Performance

Kurt Meyer: Where Can We Find Peace?

Kurt Meyer is the vice president of human resources at Methodist Health System in northwest Indiana. Kurt has more than 35 years of experience in human resources leadership and management. He views his position as critical in helping the CEO and other executives build a high-performing corporate culture. Kurt specializes in employee relations, leadership development, and talent acquisition. His commitment to enhancing the intangibles of working in healthcare is second to none.

Kurt believes that the CEO is the key to engagement. During the COVID-19 pandemic and in the post-pandemic environment, it is important for senior leadership to be viewed as genuine, compassionate, and caring. Every leader must demonstrate appreciation for the extra effort displayed by both clinicians and nonclinicians. "People are tired, nurses and other caregivers are exhausted, and they want more than pizza to feel valuable."

Human resources can create an environment in which the health of the healthcare workers is a primary goal. From values-based interviewing to ongoing recognition and support, the organization's human resources must be led and managed with the same focus and discipline as the financial resources. Kurt is focused on the "soul" of the organization: Where can we find peace in this complex and difficult time in healthcare? He believes that he and the other senior executives must be visible through rounding, helping staff with specific issues, and constantly modeling the organization's core values—that is, consistently demonstrating the culture-based behaviors expected of all employees. Kurt believes that

(continued)

(continued from previous page)

the strength of the organization's culture is a good indicator of the degree of employee engagement.

Scott Nygaard: Trust Makes Decision-Making More Efficient

For the last ten years, Scott Nygaard, MD, has worked at Lee Health in Fort Myers, Florida, where he has served in a number of roles, including chief operating officer. He brings the unique combination of medical and business expertise to the issue of employee engagement. Dr. Nygaard sees the issue as "culture—it's about the people." To that end, Scott views communication as the most critical leadership role: "We need to have critical conversations. We need to build trust."

Scott presents an interesting point of view: "The dialogue is the work!" He is committed to solving complex problems by having difficult conversations to determine the best collective decision. Scott sees that sometimes the person in charge wants to be right and therefore short-circuits any dialogue that might prove them wrong. The difficulty in using crucial conversations and collective decision-making is time. But Scott believes that when trust among the decision makers is high, there is less need for extended conversations. When trust is strong, participants are more likely to be open and honest. Scott firmly believes that a trusting environment makes the decision-making process significantly more efficient.

SUMMARY

A large universe of professional and organizational techniques can be used to create and sustain employee engagement. This chapter suggested some of the more common and easy processes and techniques that apply to healthcare organizations. The employee engagement model presented in this text begins with aligned values. Without aligned values, engagement becomes a function of personal idiosyncrasies and financial incentives. This chapter showed how aligning values begins with employment ads, followed by value-based interviewing for selection and, finally, culturally relevant behavioral onboarding. Values alignment sets the stage for meaningful work. When employees can see how their specific tasks contribute to the achievement of the corporate vision, then the tasks have meaning.

The highest form of engagement is achieved when employees find purpose in their work. Finding purpose in work is a function of the organization's mission. The mission statement articulates the reason the organization exists. Some people regard the mission as the "essence" of the organization or even refer to the mission as the organization's "soul." Organizations can, and should, review and change their vision as market forces demand; however, if the organization changes its mission, then it becomes a new organization. This chapter recommends processes and techniques that help move employees from meaningful work to finding purpose in their profession.

QUESTIONS FOR ASSESSMENT AND DISCUSSION

Thinking about your own organization, respond to the following statements on a scale of 1 to 5, where 5 = strongly agree, 4 = agree, 3 = uncertain, 2 = disagree, and 1 = strongly disagree.

1. Everyone knows how their job fits into and supports our mission, values, and vision.
2. Specific behaviors are established for each value.
3. Our corporate culture guides the process of advertising, interviewing, selecting, and promoting employees.

4. Everyone in this organization can describe who we are and what we stand for.

5. The board of trustees' agenda always includes a discussion of organizational cultural.

REFERENCES

Csikszentmihalyi, M. 2003. *Good Business: Leadership Flow and the Making of Meaning.* New York: Penguin.

———. 1993. *The Evolving Self: A Psychology for the Third Millennium.* New York: HarperCollins.

Lynn, A. B. 2008. *The EQ Interview: Finding Employees with High Emotional Intelligence.* New York: American Management Association.

CHAPTER 9

What Can Go Wrong

Failure is simply the opportunity to begin again,
this time more intelligently.
—Henry Ford

Fall seven times and stand up eight.
—Japanese proverb

Do not judge me by my successes, judge me by how many times
I fell down and got back up again.
—Nelson Mandela

THE PITFALLS OF CREATING SUSTAINABLE EMPLOYEE ENGAGEMENT

So far, this book has shown a sequential developmental model that healthcare leaders can use to increase the likelihood of sustainable employee engagement. The first eight chapters discussed the foundational elements of the model: aligned values; a vision that makes work meaningful; and the organization's mission as the source of employees' purpose. Each element is associated with specific skills that leaders can use to enhance employee engagement. Aligned values are best achieved with clear recruitment, selection, onboarding, and re-recruitment processes. Leadership and corporate culture can help employees experience meaningful work. And, the way in which the mission is communicated throughout the organization will drive the degree to which employees experience purposeful employment.

Sometimes, however, the desired outcome of sustainable employee engagement is not achieved. This chapter will discuss some of the things that can go wrong in striving toward a highly engaged workforce.

JIM COLLINS GOT IT RIGHT—PART I

Jim Collins is arguably today's best writer on leadership and organizational effectiveness. In his classic book *Good to Great* (2001), Collins outlines the characteristics of high-performing organizations and the traits of the most successful leaders, whom he calls "Level 5" leaders. Based on his research, Collins (2001, 12) summarizes his main conclusion: "We expected that good-to-great leaders would begin by setting a new vision and strategy. We found instead that they *first* got the right people on the bus, the wrong people off the bus, and the right people in the right seats—*then* they figured out where to drive it. The old adage 'People are your most important asset' turns out to be wrong. People are *not* your most important asset. The *right* people are."

Several lessons are embedded in Collins's conclusion, but for the sake of this chapter, let's focus on what can go wrong. First: The wrong people are on the bus. Exhibit 9.1 illustrates one way to assess who are the "right" and the "wrong" people.

It is important to note that when judging the "right" and "wrong" people, we are in no way judging their qualities as a human being. The judgment is based solely on the behaviors they display compared with the behavioral expectations of their job. The "right" people perform the expected behaviors at a consistently high level, whereas, the "wrong" people do not meet the performance expectations of the job.

Exhibit 9.1 The "Right" and "Wrong" People for Your Organization

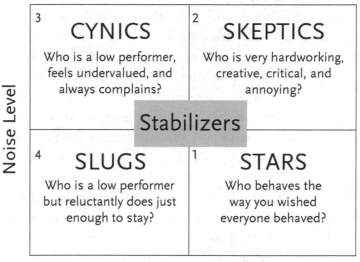

There is a concept in psychotherapy that states "Love the person, hate the behavior." In today's workplace, it is important to be sensitive to many variables, but behavior is the one that is non-negotiable. If a surgeon is a wonderful person, a leading member of the community, and a super parent, but has high surgical mortality and a morbidity rate three times the national average, then that behavior must be addressed. The highest level of leadership is the ability to separate an individual's behavior from other factors such as age, gender, race, sexuality, ethnicity, and so on.

A simple metaphor can help us understand the importance of separating an individual's behavior from other characteristics. Parenting requires identifying and rewarding the best behaviors in children based on their family history, culture, and beliefs. However, if the child's behavior deviates significantly from the parents' expectations of what is desirable, then the parent will typically intervene and redirect the child's behavior and may even punish the child. Remember, love the person, hate the behavior—parents love their children so much that they want their child to display only the best behaviors.

In terms of what can go wrong, let's look at exhibit 9.1, which can help identify the "right" and "wrong" people for your organization.

In chapter 8, we discussed the importance of identifying the A, B, and C performers, based on behaviors compared with expectations. The grid shown in exhibit 9.1 is another way to determine the "right" and "wrong" people for your bus. The horizontal axis represents the employee's contribution to performance, with low performance on the left and high performance on the right. The vertical axis indicates the "noise level," with low volume on the bottom and high volume on the top.

The bottom-right cell (1) includes high performers who are not noisy. These are the organizational "stars"—the organization's A players. The top-right cell (2) also includes high performers, but those who like to question and challenge expectations. These employees are the "skeptics." Both stars and skeptics are high performers, but the difference is the amount of emotional energy it takes to work with them. Skeptics can be exhausting. The top-left cell (3) includes low performers who complain constantly. These employees are the "cynics." Finally, the bottom-left cell (4) includes low performers who are quiet. These are the "slugs." Stars and skeptics are both high performers, but they have very different roles to play in organization growth. Cynics and slugs are both low performers, but they have significantly different impacts on the organization.

Each cell in exhibit 9.1 includes a question. Think of the people you work with and ask each question. For example, cell 1 asks, "Who is currently *behaving* the way you wished everyone *behaved*?" The individuals who come to mind are your "stars." After asking the questions in each cell, you'll find that some employees don't fit into any of the four cells. These employees are "stabilizers." They are good (but not great) workers who don't complain but execute the required behaviors consistently. Anecdotal evidence suggests that the number of stars in any organization is roughly the square root of the total number of staff. For example, if you are the director of a department with 100 employees, you probably have about 10 stars. The number of skeptics tends to vary depending on profession. Although physicians tend to have more skeptics among them, skeptics typically make up 10 to 12 percent of any population. Cynics usually account for only 3 to 5 percent of any population, but because they are so noisy—these are the complainers and naysayers—it might seem like there are many more. Finally, the slugs tend to make up 3 to 5 percent of the workers in an organization.

Understanding the difference between the stars and the skeptics is critical, especially during times of rapid change. The stars are the highest performers in the organization. They consistently display exceptional performance. However, the stars are not a good resource for innovation. New ideas are found by working with the skeptics. While the stars perform tasks at a very high level, the skeptics are thinking about a dozen different ways to accomplish the desired goal. The skeptics are most successful at generating new ideas. A useful process for leading a change process is to challenge the skeptics to come up with some ideas for a better future, then take those ideas to the stars for implementation. In his book *Leading Change* (1996), John Kotter presents the idea of a "guiding coalition." The purpose of this small group of high performers is to lead others through the change process.

Understanding the difference between the cynics and the slugs is also important to avoid the "what can go wrong?" trap. The cynics are individuals who are never happy. When they get a pay raise, their response is "It should have been more," or "It sure took them long enough to give us something," or "I'll bet the CEO got a lot more than we did." These individuals are impossible to engage in the values, vision, and mission. They are always thinking about themselves ("What's in it for me?") or playing the victim ("They always are picking on me!"). In an organization, cynics are skilled at pulling others into their "negative vortex of doom"! Their negative verbal behavior is toxic to the rest of the staff. The damage that cynics can do is even greater when they are in management positions. Slugs, on the other hand, don't want to be noticed. These individuals do just enough to not get fired: They take all of their personal and sick time, and they are the last to arrive for work and the first to leave. Slugs are essentially harmless—except they occupy positions (and take paychecks) from others who might be stars.

How do leaders handle these four types of workers? The stars need to be re-recruited. The skeptics need to be encouraged to generate new ideas. The cynics need to be fired. And the slugs need to be challenged to increase their productivity or given an opportunity to resign.

A note about firing the cynics: Removing toxic employees is critical to ensure the overall health of the organization. However, remember that the decision rule for classifying someone is their behavior. Termination must be based on behaviorally specific—absolutely objective—data on the individual's performance measured against the expected behavior. Termination cannot be based on subjective criteria. Collins's process of "getting the right people on the bus and the wrong people off the bus" must be guided by the principle of "love the person, hate the behavior." Sadly, managers sometimes need to get mad at an individual before dealing with their aberrant behavior. However, this reaction introduces subjectivity and emotion into what should be a clear process of eliminating unacceptable behavior.

COLLINS GOT IT RIGHT—PART 2

"Get the right people in the right seats." Laurence J. Peter first described his "Peter Principle" in 1969. The premise is that, whenever there is an organizational hierarchy, people tend to rise to their "level of incompetency." Talent management in healthcare is one of today's most critical leadership skills. When the stars have been identified, how do you re-recruit them without promoting them to their level of incompetence?

Let's consider the example of Bob, an outstanding nurse manager with master's degrees in nursing and business administration. Bob was the senior nurse manager for all inpatient services in a large tertiary hospital. The pay scale in this hospital was based on longevity and academic credentials. Because Bob had worked there a long time and held the highest credentials, there was no way to increase Bob's salary under this system. Therefore, the hospital's senior executives decided to make Bob a system vice president so that he could benefit from a new pay and benefit plan.

Bob's personality could be described as timid. Although he was exceptionally bright, his thinking process was linear. His decisions were based solely on data. These traits made him an exceptional nurse manager. However, they were not the traits he needed to succeed as a system vice president. As a nurse manager, Bob could make planning and budgeting decisions using data. He was comfortable not having to deal with a lot of "people" issues, only clinical issues. But as a system vice president, his linear thinking and data-driven style were inadequate to his position; he needed to develop a nonlinear, more collaborative style in which the influence of peers and local managers was key to his success. Bob failed miserably.

What senior leadership did was take an outstanding manager and put him in a position in which his talents were ineffective. The system's leadership had a thoughtful, considerate, and genuine positive goal—find a way to reward Bob financially. But the leadership "put the wrong person in the wrong seat," to use Collins's analogy. And, to make matters worse, because of Bob's incompetence as a vice president, the leadership planned to terminate his employment. Fortunately, hospital leadership offered Bob executive coaching; that process made clear that Bob had never wanted to leave his nurse management position—he only did so because of the higher paycheck. Bob returned to his management position and, the story goes, lived happily ever after.

Bob's story contains several lessons. First, promoting an employee to their level of incompetence can be disastrous. In this case, the hospital lost a great manager, and the system added an incompetent executive. The second lesson is more subtle: People will make poor decisions if the money is attractive enough. The challenge for the system was how to recognize, reward, and re-recruit a high performer (a star or A player) without removing him from the position in which he produces the most value.

COLLINS GOT IT RIGHT—PART 3: NARCISSISTS CANNOT LEAD

A narcissist can be described as someone who has an inflated sense of their own importance, a deep need for attention and admiration, and a lack of empathy. As a result of these qualities, narcissists often have troubled relationships. Remember, leaders have followers because of the empathetic and trusting relationships they develop over time. However, when an individual views all events through the lens of what is best for me, it is impossible to inspire followers.

In healthcare today, there are many examples of senior executives, physicians, and sometimes trustees who fall into the narcissist category. The modus operandi of such individuals is to never accept blame and always find a scapegoat; to take credit for successes and avoid any responsibility for failures; and to surround themselves with sycophants who enable their behavior. These individuals often rise to senor executive positions because of their business or clinical skills. However, because their decision-making is based on "what's the best outcome for me?," they are unable to figure out what direction to "drive the bus." These individuals have short-term, opportunistic planning cycles that can change overnight. They are more toxic than cynics in terms of creating and sustaining employee engagement. They view all intangible, people-oriented processes as "touchy-feely" and believe they have nothing to do with "hitting the numbers."

Here is a real-life example of such an executive. A small two-hospital, multi-clinic system in a midwestern state replaced a long-term veteran CEO with a younger individual from one of the coasts. The new CEO was tall, handsome, glib, charming, and, behind the scenes, ruthless. His two main foci were absolute loyalty and making the budget. In terms of loyalty, he terminated several executives who thought he was serious when he asked for their input. If he didn't like their feedback, he found a way to replace them. Within six months, he had assembled a team of sycophants.

This CEO's narcissistic behaviors and his inability to create a vision of "where to drive the bus" corrupted the healthcare system. His most egregious act was to terminate—two weeks before Christmas—60 full-time employees, most of whom were direct care providers. By doing so, the system made its annual budget and rewarded the CEO with a $150,000 bonus.

The fallout was predictable: The physicians, many of whom had lost their longtime providers, were furious, and morale tanked. But, like all narcissists, the CEO put all of the blame on his human resources professionals—"they gave him faulty data!" He terminated the vice president of human resources.

Sadly, this individual is still in his CEO role. The trustees think he is great, because he always makes the budget. He holds strict control over the data that the trustees see, and, not surprisingly, he eliminated employee and physician engagement surveys, calling them "an unnecessary cost that only produces that 'touchy-feely' data that has nothing to do with running the business." However, to comply with the requirements of licensing agencies, he collects survey data the week after pay increases. A cynic might posit that he is trying to influence the outcome!

WHAT CAN GO WRONG: LOSING STARS

Losing a star is much more than losing one full-time employee. When a company loses a star for avoidable reasons, it has lost an important part of its culture—a piece of its soul. And, when a star leaves unexpectedly, the departure is noticed by many, if not all, employees. Several reasons can cause serious but preventable organizational "wrongs." Together, they can have a major impact on employee engagement.

One of the most destructive dynamics that erodes engagement is the perception of favoritism. When a star sees that they are getting an unusual amount of responsibility and a coworker is able to "dog it," the star's motivation decreases greatly. In line with this dynamic is a common but especially insidious dynamic. There is a common aphorism: "If you want something done, give it to a busy person." In toxic work environments, managers continue to give the stars more work because they know that the work will be done. The manager increases the star's workload instead of replacing the cynics and slugs. After a while, the star realizes that no amount of effort will ever alter their work assignments and quits. It is an accepted reality that employees don't leave an organization, they leave their boss. Losing stars, for whatever reason, is a serious and ultimately fatal wrong.

Profiles of Performance

John Smith: The Antithesis of the Employee Engagement Model

John Smith is a 53-year-old white man who has been the CEO of Acme General Hospital for 17 years. He earned a bachelor's degree in business in 1988 and a master of health administration degree in 1993. He takes great pride in the fact that he has not attended any academic or nonmandated professional development programs since completing his degree. He has never pursued the FACHE (Fellow of the American College of Healthcare Executives) credential, arguing that leaders who use letters after their name for status are not worth his time. John is a classic "Theory X" executive. Had he taken the time to read a few books on organizational dynamics, he would know that Theory X executives are toxic and that they ultimately fail.

Theory X, and its opposite, Theory Y, were proposed by Douglas McGregor in the 1950s (McGregor 1960). Theory X holds that the typical worker is lazy, has no ambition, is selfish, and avoids responsibility. Because of these innate,

(continued)

(continued from previous page)

unchangeable characteristics, all employees must be controlled with the "carrot and stick"—with heavy emphasis on the stick. Theory X is often compared with Theory Y. Theory Y is based on the opposite assumptions about workers. According to Theory Y, the typical worker is self-motived, hardworking, and looking to advance though effort and education. Of course, there is no place for such workers in John Smith's hospital.

John's most notable characteristic is hubris. He believes that his management style is the reason for the hospital's success. He discounts the unusual market dynamics that placed him in a highly attractive location with many self-insured businesses, health-conscious community members, and little competition. The hospital's financial success allows John to pay above-market salaries to executives. His strategy is to pay good salaries with very large bonuses to executives if their departments "hit their numbers" (the carrot), but if they miss their financial targets for two reporting periods, they are replaced (the stick). John's "management by walking about" is focused only on departments that are not performing to his standard of success—profit.

The hospital's physicians have, for the most part, resisted employment contracts—they can see what happens to employees. The largest multispecialty group took it upon itself to engage a consultant to help create a program to implement best practices, data-driven quality improvement, and positive patient experiences. All of the local attending physicians were invited to an initial planning session. More than 90 percent of the physicians participated. The meeting ended with the creation of a group charter, a timeline, and a 12-person task force to move the project forward. After three months of

(continued)

(continued from previous page)

concentrated and productive work, the task force was ready to present its work product to the CEO and, it hoped, to the board of trustees.

An evening meeting was set to accommodate the CEO's schedule. The meeting was held at the nicest hotel in town, with an elegant catered buffet and top-shelf drinks (all paid for by the physicians). The CEO arrived an hour late, without apology, and headed straight for the buffet and bar. The chief of staff welcomed the CEO, introduced the attendees, and explained the purpose of the task force and its hope that its work product would become a significant part of the hospital's quality improvement process and patient experience strategy.

The CEO listened while finishing his dinner and cocktail, then stated, in a patronizing tone, that he was happy that the physicians were working on how "they" could improve their patient care. He then stood and said that his wife wanted to look at a new house, and "making his wife happy was more important than listening to physicians talk about their patient issues." However, he could meet with their consultant tomorrow morning, and the consultant could present the task force's findings. Then he left.

The physicians' emotions ranged from anger to frustration to apathy. An intense three-month process led by highly engaged physician leaders ended with a whimper, not a bang. The consultant asked for advice on what to say to the CEO the next morning. After the meeting, the consultant, chief of staff, and two other physician leaders stayed for another hour to discuss how best to approach the CEO. They decided to show the CEO the large binder containing the complete work product, but mainly to present a one-page executive

(continued)

(continued from previous page)

summary of their work and recommendations for next steps. The consultants and the chief of staff agreed to meet after the presentation to the CEO.

The meeting with the CEO could not have been more disastrous. First, the CEO made the consultant wait 15 minutes before starting the meeting. The consultant thanked the CEO for his time and presented the binder and executive summary for discussion. The CEO put these materials aside and launched into a diatribe about how he ran the hospital and no physicians or consultants were going to tell him what to do. He shouted that he was offended that they had made him come to a dinner meeting to try to manipulate him. And, as far as he was concerned, "physicians are overpaid animals and needed to be caged." He then summarily dismissed the consultant and said that he hoped he never showed up at "his" hospital again. The consultant left the executive, with noticeably higher blood pressure, and went to debrief the chief of staff. The chief of staff was frustrated and angry, but not that surprised.

The CEO felt that he had handled the "rogue physicians" masterfully, and all of his executives agreed. But inside this bubble, the CEO never thought about the fact that each of the hospital's trustees went to one or more of these physicians for their own healthcare. Many of the physicians also belonged to the same country clubs and places of worship. The chief of staff called a meeting at his home that included the senior physicians and the executive committee of the board. The consultant joined the meeting by phone. Just before midnight, the decision was made that the CEO needed to be terminated. A week of follow-up meetings among the physicians, trustees, and legal counsel ended with a termination agreement and timeline for the CEO's departure.

(continued)

(continued from previous page)

The CEO meet with the executive committee and legal counsel at a Friday afternoon "emergency" meeting. Needless to say, the CEO was shocked, surprised, and angry that the board had been manipulated by a few rogue physicians. He threatened lawsuits for wrongful termination and slander. The board chair noted that it was his right to sue, but doing so would negate the generous termination agreement, which included a face-saving retirement celebration. The board suggested he take the weekend to consider his options, but, regardless of his decision to sue, he was no longer the CEO. On Monday, he accepted the termination agreement and signed the lawyer-created letter of resignation. Interestingly, when the CEO left for the last time, the only sounds that could be heard throughout the hospital were cheers and applause!

Note: John Smith's leadership style is an amalgamation of three of the most toxic healthcare CEOs in this consultant's experience. But the description of the physician-led quality improvement work and the CEO's response is true—as is the CEO's termination and the resulting joy throughout the hospital.

SUMMARY

Employee engagement in healthcare delivery is a complicated process that must consider the wide range of needs and interests of an employee population with diverse professional, generational, ethnic, racial, and other unique human characteristics. Regardless of these variables, a few immutable organizational dynamics exist. Employees want to be valued, they want to be respected, they want to control parts of the decisions that most affect their work, and they want to grow professionally. Many things can go wrong in creating a culture of sustainable employee engagement. This chapter has shown some of the most egregious.

All of the things that can go wrong with employee engagement can be easily identified in one or more of the four elements of the model presented in this book. But there is one notable factor that controls the degree of employee engagement: the CEO's leadership style. Is the person sitting in the CEO's office a leader—does that person inspire followers? Or, is the CEO just a very highly paid individual who is interested in themselves above all else? The individuals featured in the Profiles of Performance throughout this book are all leaders. In fact, they all fall into the "Level 5 leader" category described by Jim Collins. On the other hand, John Smith, showcased in this chapter's performance profile, is the antithesis of leadership—under no circumstances would he be able to create a positive corporate culture that fosters sustainable employee engagement. Sometimes it is useful to study the negative to learn the behavioral limits to which no leader should aspire.

QUESTIONS FOR ASSESSMENT AND DISCUSSION

1. Are our decisions about employees based on Theory X or Theory Y?
2. Do we know who are the stars, skeptics, cynics, and slugs in our organization?
3. Do we "mine" the skeptics for innovative ideas?
4. Do we work with our stars to lead change process?
5. Are we guilty of the implementing the "Peter principle"?

REFERENCES

Collins, J. C. 2001. *Good to Great: Why Some Companies Make the Leap and Others Don't*. New York: Harper Business.

Kotter, J. P. 1996. *Leading Change*. Boston: Harvard Business School Press.

McGregor, D. 1960. *The Human Side of Enterprise*. New York: McGaw-Hill.

Peter, L. J. 1969. *The Peter Principle*. New York: Harper Business.

CHAPTER 10

Putting It All Together

*Start with good people, lay out the rules, communicate
with your employees, motivate them and reward them.
If you do all of these things effectively, you can't miss.*
—Lee Iacocca

*An organization's ability to learn, and translate that learning into
action, is the ultimate competitive advantage.*
—Jack Welch

Open your arms to change but don't let go of your values.
—Dalai Lama

A CASE STUDY

Utopia Health (UH) was incorporated four years ago. UH is a
unique global network designed primarily for population health
and other "healthy humans" service components. UH is connected
electronically to dozens of countries, thousands of facilities, and
tens of thousands of healthcare providers and staff. UH has a strong
corporate culture based on its mission, core values, and vision.

- **Mission.** Utopia Health exists to be the main resource on
the planet Earth for health, wellness, disease management,
sickness, death with dignity, and trauma recovery.

- **Core values.** Excellence, caring, service, innovation, and empathy
  - Excellence: Strive to exceed best practices criteria in all clinical and business activities
  - Caring: Demonstrate human touch in all interactions with those we serve
  - Service: We are here to meet and exceed expectations
  - Innovation: Use the best and most current technological tools and discoveries in all we do
  - Empathy: Show a deep understanding of others' feelings, condition, hopes, and experiences
- **Vision.** In the next 10 years, UH will be the best worldwide healthcare resource and a partner for all people who have a desire to live to their full health potential.

UH is a global corporation representing a network of several countries. Because of the legal requirements of operating in each country, its governance structure is complicated. The parent board has 12 members and includes international board members. There is a trustee from Dubai, one from the United Kingdom, one from Singapore, and one from Brazil. The international reach of UH's services requires input from around the globe. The CEO is a voting member of the board and serves as vice chair. Two physicians and two nurses are full voting members of the board. Board members serve on a rotating three-year schedule. The remaining board members are selected from the Foundation Board. The Foundation Board is a much larger board of international members who assist with fundraising but act as a sounding-board and resource for the parent board.

UH was started in the United States, and its main office is located in Austin, Texas. Other offices are located in Dubai, Singapore, London, Rio de Janeiro, Tel Aviv, Sydney, and Cape Town. The initial 10-year capitalization was acquired from several individuals and governments. For example, in the United States, investors include

Elon Musk, Jeff Bezos, the Koch brothers, the Gates Foundation, the Walton family, Warren Buffett, and many other smaller investors. On the international front, Mohammed bin Rashid Al Maktoum from Dubai is an investor and trustee, as is the prime minister of Singapore, Lee Hsien Loong. Board members are designated from the United Kingdom and Brazil.

UH's CEO, Elise Castro, was hired as soon as the corporation was established. Castro came to the healthcare industry after several years with an international consulting company. Her knowledge of and experience with the global impact of big data, predictive analytics, and artificial intelligence (AI) were a big part of the board's decision to hire her. Her academic and work history, while important, was only part of the reason Castro was hired as CEO. During interviews, she made a statement that was significant in helping the board make its decision. Castro strongly believes that "my job as a leader is not to create followers, but rather to create more leaders." She often states that "healthcare is not a business for people." Rather, healthcare is "a people business—people always come first." Castro strikes a balance between the linear, tangible business realities and the nonlinear, intangible human realities. Castro is CEO of UH's parent company, but each partner nation has its own corporate infrastructure.

Among the many books that Castro has read about high-performing organizations, the one that had the most impact on her was Patrick Lencioni's *The Four Obsessions of an Extraordinary Executive* (2000). The "four obsessions" described by Lencioni (2000, 141) are "(1) build and maintain a cohesive leadership team; (2) create organizational clarity; (3) overcommunicate clarity; (4) reinforce clarity through human systems."

Castro began her job by building a cohesive leadership team from diverse backgrounds. She first created an Office of the President, which she views as a "five-headed," highly collaborative team of skilled and highly trusted individuals with exceptionally high emotional intelligence. Her team consists of the chief medical officer (CMO), Dr. Lucas Robert, a brilliant cardiovascular surgeon and self-taught informatics expert; the chief nursing officer (CNO),

Juliana Courtney, whose doctoral dissertation focused on population health; the chief financial officer (CFO), Susanne Washington, an exceptional finance officer with several years of experience in international finance who is also the treasurer of the corporation; and the chief people officer (CPO), Dr. Amil Kahn, who has studied and written extensively on cognitive psychology and innovations in adult learning. Dr. Kahn has engineered an exceptionally effective global learning system based on virtual reality and augmented reality. Dr. Kahn's approach to lifelong learning is just one example of how Castro and her team intend to lead a highly successful health company in today's "gig" environment.

These five professionals make up the Office of the President and work as a senior leadership team. The corporate office in Austin has few employees. The bulk of the work is done remotely. Thousands of information technology experts from across the globe are the "engine" that makes UH work. The Office of the President's daily job is to discuss different points of view, embrace dynamic tension, commit to the best decisions, and, most importantly, hold everyone accountable for meeting the global mission.

Castro believes that by having the CMO and CNO as equal members of the leadership team, the best clinical, preventative, and population health decisions can be made. She also believes that the traditional human resources function has become bogged down by labor rules and regulations, pay and benefits policies, and employee issues. So, she created the position of chief people officer, to whom the traditional vice president of human resources reports. The CPO is responsible for all employee-related policies and activities, such as recruitment, selection, re-recruitment, onboarding, professional development, reward and recognition systems, and employee engagement. Just as the CMO and CNO work closely together on clinical issues, the CPO and CFO work closely on human capital and financial capital issues.

The Office of the President meets every morning, either in person or electronically, to discuss one question: What can we do today to better serve our staff and the people who depend on us for their health? The leadership team begins every day by following Lencioni's second obsession: "create organizational clarity." They select one target for each core value and then follow Lencioni's third and fourth obsessions: overcommunicate clarity and reinforce through human systems. The leadership team "overcommunicates" cultural expectations to its international partners with the understanding that information and expectations will flow throughout the global organization. The most important step in maintaining a high-performing international organization is to enlist every piece of the network in showing how their work helps meet the principal challenges. Castro and her team know that when this happens, everyone throughout the global network is fully engaged.

UH is unique in several ways. It does not own or manage any hospitals, clinics, physician practices, pharmacies, or any other physical component needed to deliver care, treat trauma, or assist with maximizing population health. A simple analogy is that UH is an Amazon or an Uber for healthcare. Because of its massive investments in AI, big data, and predictive analytics, UH is able to align the services needed to maximize health down to the individual. The actual care is provided by a complicated network of providers worldwide. Costs are minimized through competition. If someone in Montana or Honduras, for example, needs a particular intervention, that person goes to UH's website to find out whether it can be done electronically via telemedicine or to learn where to get high-quality care in person. If a patient needs in-person care, the best provider of that service in the world is available with a "one-click purchase." The database assigns a price for the service based on the person's ability to pay, and the rest is covered by UH's global members.

The first ten years of UH's international agreement were designed to discover whether AI, big data, and predictive analytics could be organized into a global network to care for the sick and disabled and to maximize population health. With six years left on the agreement, some positive outcomes have already been achieved. For example, international competition has lowered the costs of many interventions and medications. Hospital beds are more appropriately tied to need. End-of-life concerns are being addressed with greater human compassion and respect because everyone has read and operationalized Dr. Atul Gawande's thoughts in his book *Being Mortal: Medicine and What Matters in the End* (2017). In the next six years, even greater health, wellness, and compassionate end-of-life experiences will be developed. Many new and exciting opportunities are emerging as a result of quantum computing, machine learning, robotics, genomics, and nanotechnologies. Cloud computing will continue to evolve, allowing UH to integrate new discoveries into its global model of care. At some point, UH could be able to provide an individual health plan for every one of the more than seven billion people on the planet.

BACK TO TODAY'S REALITY

Utopia Health, of course, is pure fantasy. However, many of the notions included in this description are very real today. Technological discoveries continue at a rapid pace. Many of these discoveries have the potential to replace tasks currently completed by workers. What happens when robots displace workers? What happens when discoveries are made that cure cancer, or at least make it a manageable condition, like diabetes? Employee engagement, commitment, and loyalty will continue to be challenges within today's and tomorrow's healthcare delivery structure. Will we see the evolution of an Amazon- or Uber-type business model in which healthcare providers have more control over the decisions that affect them? Will there ever be a "one-click" opportunity to control our own health? Will the evolving healthcare delivery models be structured so that providers are valued for their contributions, and so that all who are involved in the delivery of care, including business support staff, are developed to their full potential?

Utopia Health does not exist currently, but imagine the total level of engagement if everything one did everyday had a direct, positive impact on the health and well-being of the people on this planet—a global sense of purpose. In the last few decades, we have experienced transformational changes driven by technology—the internet, the iPhone, Amazon, electric cars, and private space travel, just to name a few. It is reasonable to believe that at some point, technology will transform the delivery of healthcare in the United States, and possibly beyond our borders.

One of the lessons of the COVID-19 pandemic and post-pandemic care models is that healthcare providers are universally committed to helping others. During and after the pandemic, healthcare workers were hailed as heroes, saving lives while putting themselves at risk. Executive leadership during this time was focused on "What needs to be done today to help our providers do their job?" In other words, people serving people—a simple statement, almost a "bumper sticker," but nonetheless cogent, relevant, and critical to the sustainable engagement of providers in a viable and healthy organization. Healthcare leaders who focus on the "health" of their delivery system will be rewarded with the most sustainable employee engagement.

In their book *Patients Come Second*, Paul Spiegelman and Britt Berrett (2018, 6) present the controversial argument that healthcare leaders should focus on employees first and patients second: "What do you mean that 'patients come second'? Why would you focus on your employees if you want to improve the experience of the patient? Sounds like you guys must have written yourselves an extra prescription or two. Well, while we admit to being somewhat wacky and fun loving, we're stiff-lipped serious when it comes to the notion that an organization's culture—specifically, how engaged its employees are in their work—is the primary driver for delivering an exceptional patient experience."

Spiegelman and Berrett's focus on the employee reinforces the message of this book: Employees must be able to work in a healthy organization that has a strong corporate culture based on core values that are shared by everyone; an organization that has an inspirational, directional, and measurable vision in which workers can find meaning; and an organization that has a mission statement that allows employees to find purpose in their connection to the mission.

This book has put forth a model that, when implemented sequentially, will create these factors and produce sustainable employee engagement.

The desired result of a highly engaged workforce begins with aligning individual workers' values with the organization's core corporate values. Without aligned values, the probability of sustainable employee engagement is zero. An organization in which employees' values are in conflict with corporate values can only create episodic engagement with external rewards (money) or punishment (the threat of termination).

The second step in the sustainable engagement process is to tie workers' tasks to the achievement of the organization's vision. An organization's vision is a time-specific picture of a desirable future. Employees find meaning in their work when they see how their roles and responsibilities directly contribute to the achievement of the vision. The highest level of connection to the organization is achieved when employees view their work as a calling. They find purpose in their contribution to the mission.

High-performing organizations with engaged employees are led by genuine leaders. Low-performing organizations with disengaged employees are not led but managed by people with big titles and paychecks, but no followers. Take a look at exhibit 10.1, which lists the traits of high- and low-performing organizations. One useful application of these traits is a self-assessment of both your individual leadership and the organization's priorities.

Healthcare is an industry in which people take care of people. However, over the past few decades, we have seen the erosion of the deep personal relationship between the patient and the caregiver. Increases in mandates, rules, and regulations that control the performance expectations and financing of healthcare have, in many ways, driven a wedge between the patient and the provider. The electronic medical record is one example of how technology has affected care delivery. It is easy to image a future when even more technology will be inserted into care delivery systems to improve quality, data collection, and performance consistency.

Exhibit 10.1 Traits of High- and Low-Performing Organizations

HIGH-PERFORMING ORGANIZATION

FACTOR	TRAITS
CLO Chief leadership officer	• Competency • Integrity • Consistency • Courage • Humility
Positive workplace environment	• Meaningful work • Professional development • Respect • Clear direction • Reasonable expectations
Followers	• Pride • Joy • Engaged • Innovative • Rewarded

LOW-PERFORMING ORGANIZATION

FACTOR	TRAITS
CTO Chief titled officer	• Economic focus • Egocentric behavior • Overcontrolling • Unpredictable • Autocratic
Toxic workplace environment	• Productivity measures rule • High stress • Expectations change often • Employees are viewed as economic units • No/limited opportunity for professional development
Survivors	• Minimum behavior • Blame transfer • Avoidance • Uncertainty • Anger (passive-aggressive behavior)

During this evolution to greater use of AI, big data, and predictive analytics, healthcare leaders must be sure that the workforce is connected to the vision and the mission. Healthcare leadership's greatest responsibility is to create a strong corporate culture that allows all employees to find meaning and purpose in their work. This culture must be the basis for sustainable engagement. Because of the increasing pressures involved in healthcare delivery, the culture must also provide for workers' mental and physical health. The board of trustees must play a significant role is ensuring that the organization is fostering maximum employee engagement.

THE TRUSTEE'S ROLE IN EMPLOYEE ENGAGEMENT

The first and most important group of people responsible for creating and maintaining a culture of sustainable engagement is the board of trustees. When governance is clear that the organization's mission, values, and vision are the "North Star" for all decisions, there is greater likelihood that such a corporate culture will be created.

In a thoughtful piece for *Boardroom Press*, the monthly journal of the Governance Institute, Ryan Donohue (2020) offers valuable advice for healthcare trustees. Donohue lists a number of "key board takeaways" for rethinking employee engagement, such as establishing a standing board committee on employee engagement. Such a committee should be staffed by the chief people officer. A small but symbolic way to demonstrate the importance of employee engagement is to have this committee present its data before the financial data presentation. A key element of the board of trustees' responsibilities is to functionally define what employee engagement looks like in the organization. Too often, it is assumed that employee engagement is universally understood. However, the most effective organizations have behaviorally specific descriptions of employee engagement, and these descriptions are usually tied to their values.

HEALTHY ORGANIZATIONS ALLOW FOR SUSTAINABLE EMPLOYEE ENGAGEMENT

We learned during the COVID-19 pandemic that the majority of healthcare providers can rise to any challenge. The physical, emotional, and spiritual energy that was directed at helping COVID-19 patients was exemplary, but not without human cost. Fatigue, frustration, fear, and physical exhaustion were just a few of the negative outcomes of giving everything to care for others. This fact is mentioned because this book is about how leaders create a corporate culture in which employees can find meaningful work and professional purpose. The journey from a job to a purpose can only occur within a healthy organization. Some promising research is being done on the importance of psychological safety as a critical factor in employee engagement and long-term organizational viability. Employee engagement cannot be sustained in a psychologically unsafe environment. For example, a 2021 McKinsey & Company report determined that "only a handful of business leaders often demonstrate the positive behaviors that can instill . . . psychological safety in their workforce" (De Smet et al. 2021). Psychological safety can be defined as a situation in which employees "feel comfortable asking for help, sharing suggestions informally, or challenging the status quo without fear of negative social consequences." As a result, "organizations are more likely to innovate quickly, unlock the benefits of diversity and adapt well to change." The leaders of healthy healthcare organizations embrace their employees' physical, mental, and spiritual health. Doing so makes it possible for employees to function effectively and actively engage in change processes.

The human costs of the COVID-19 pandemic have been unprecedented. Healthcare workers are in need of physical and psychological comfort. Leaders of healthy healthcare organizations must focus on the total health of employees in light of constant expectations of maximum effort. Two examples of outstanding healthcare leaders who strive daily to create a healthy work culture are Kim Miller and Karen Clements.

Profiles of Performance

Kim Miller: We Are Guided by Our Moral Compass

Kim Miller, FACHE, is the president of Western Region Baptist Health in Fort Smith, Arkansas. According to her LinkedIn bio, Kim is "known for consistent and impressive results through targeted growth of services in highly competitive markets; cultural transformation; and modeling the importance of values, ethics and integrity." She is "passionate and dedicated to a forward thinking philosophy; mentoring and investing in the growth of people as the most important asset within the organization."

During her interview for this book, Kim stated that "employee engagement for frontline workers is more important than ever." She believes that employees are "very resilient." Kim's leadership philosophy is guided by five principles. First, she wants to find ways to "show gratitude" each day for the amazing work performed by providers, healthcare workers, and business support personnel. "They are the ones who ensure our patients get the best care, and we must first take care of our employees." This principle was especially important in light of the extraordinary effort displayed during the pandemic.

Kim's second principle is to use active listening techniques when communicating with staff. Kim wants her staff to know that "I understand—I was there," "I hear what you're saying," and "I am aware of your situation, and I want to help."

Kim's third leadership principle is to be "as transparent as possible. That means I am open, honest and consistent in my messaging, because I want to build trust. Our actions must always match our words."

(continued)

(continued from previous page)

Her fourth principle concerns the mission, values, and vision of the organization. Baptist Health is a faith-based system, and its core beliefs are embedded in all communications. Kim noted that "the system aligns our service and work with the healing ministry; the work the staff does is always connected to the system's mission, core values, and the vision."

Her fifth principle is to use modern technology as much as possible to improve care delivery. But, more importantly, the use of technology must never interfere with the personal connection among providers, caregivers, patients, and families.

Kim started a program called "Caring for the Caregivers," led by a steering committee composed of leaders and employees who want to find ways to create a healthier work environment and increase employee engagement. Caregivers cannot take care of others if they do not take care of themselves. This committee works to identify ways the organization can offer support to those caring for patients. According to Kim, the organization is guided by "our moral compass."

Karen Clements: Creating an Environment for Sustainable Employee Engagement

Karen Clements, RN, FACHE, is the chief nursing officer at Dartmouth-Hitchcock Medical Center in Lebanon, New Hampshire. Karen's approach to employee engagement begins with maximizing her visibility. She wants nurses and other caregivers to "know who I am." She rounds often and uses e-mails and YouTube videos to communicate. Communication is the focal point of Karen's leadership style.

Karen's goal is to be honest, open, and available. Her personal challenge is to learn, "How do I communicate better?"

(continued)

(continued from previous page)

To this end, Karen leads a nurse corps composed of four generations. Being sensitive to differences in generational communication, she works with coaches and advisers on how best to communicate with baby boomers, Generation X, millennials, and Generation Z. Karen's goal is to increase the "connectedness" among nurses and patients, regardless of their age or experience. To reinforce this connection, Karen states, "We celebrate a lot! We give out many awards that focus on our role as nurses and caregivers within the Dartmouth-Hitchcock culture." Underpinning the nurses' work is the feeling that "We want to have fun, wherever it is appropriate."

According to the "Nursing Mission Statement" that Karen created, Dartmouth-Hitchcock nurses work every day "to advance the art and science of caring." The organization's "Nursing Vision Statement" is "To achieve nursing excellence through mentorship, research, education, evidence-based practice, and community partnerships, providing each person the best care, in the right place, at the right time, every time." Simply put, Karen's goal is to provide an environment that is "great for nurses to give care and for patients to receive care."

During the COVID-19 pandemic, Karen went the extra mile to assure nurses that their mental and physical health was important to the organization. She made rooms available for those who needed to rest. Karen delivered water, juice, and snacks to the nurses during busy times. "We did everything possible to keep morale up during the pandemic crisis."

A healthy work environment is very important to Karen. Dartmouth-Hitchcock's leadership has established a clear and public policy of "zero tolerance" for aggressive physical and/or verbal behavior directed at any staff. The system's

(continued)

(continued from previous page)

hospitals have posted large signs stating that "Dartmouth-Hitchcock Is a Healing Environment—Please Treat Others with Kindness and Respect." As part of the organization's policy, Karen implemented a nurse "zero-tolerance" process in 2018. This process includes daily huddles to discuss potential situations and to put in place proactive plans to deal with aggressive situations. Hospital security is directly involved and available to nurses whenever they are needed. Signs and posters are displayed throughout the hospital educating the public that any type of violence will not be tolerated. Hands-on training has been, and continues to be, provided to the staff. Because of these and other measures designed to keep nurses safe from violence, Karen says, "There has been a significant decrease in our workplace violence."

Karen's focus on communication, physical and mental support, rewards, fun, and personal safety has created a fertile environment for sustainable employee engagement.

SUMMARY

Will Utopia Health ever exist? Probably not. However, the next several decades will see a tremendous increase in the use of AI, big data, predictive analytics, robotics, genomics, quantum computing, and things yet unimagined. The challenge for leaders now, and in an ever-changing future, is to ensure that the human condition is advanced by these changes and not diminished. How will organizations be structured? Will we ever see a global, no-borders health and wellness system? Will personalized medicine ever become "Amazon-like," with one-click, on-demand care?

Employees in today's healthcare delivery systems have hard-wired needs that organizations must incorporate into their work processes. Employees want to be valued. They want to be challenged at work and in their professional development. They want to know that they have a future. They want to be compensated fairly. They want to work in a safe and healthy organization. To be fully engaged, they want to know that their work has meaning in terms of vision achievement, and that their work gives their lives a greater purpose because of their connection to the organization's mission.

Let's end this book with a relevant quote from Jack Welch: "There are only three measurements that tell you nearly everything you need to know about your organization's overall performance: employee engagement, customer satisfaction and cash flow. It goes without saying that no company, small or large, can win over the long run without energized employees who believe in the mission and understand how to achieve it."

QUESTIONS FOR ASSESSMENT AND DISCUSSION

1. Does the board of trustees regularly receive reports from the standing committee on employee engagement?
2. Does executive leadership have a trustee-approved zero-tolerance policy for verbal or physical violence?
3. Have the board and executive leadership created a policy, strategy, and metrics for a healthy work environment?
4. Are employees and human factors considered in technology rollouts?
5. Do we consider how to strengthen our employee engagement as part of our daily planning?

REFERENCES

DeSmet, A., K. Rubenstein, G. Schrab, M. Vierow, and A. Edmondson. 2021. "Psychological Safety and the Critical Role of Leadership." McKinsey & Company. Published February 11. www.mckinsey.com/business-functions/organization/our-insights/psychological-safety-and-the-critical-role-of-leadership-development.

Donohue, R. 2020. "Employee Engagement: What Is the Board's Role?" *Boardroom Press*. Published February. www.governanceinstitute.com/global_engine/download.aspx?fileid=78B9A857-6D3F-4D5A-806A-D1C6A899BBDC.

Gawande, A. 2017. *Being Mortal: Medicine and What Matters in the End*. New York: Picador.

Lencioni, P. K. 2000. *The Four Obsessions of an Extraordinary Executive*. San Francisco: Jossey-Bass.

Spiegelman, P., and B. Berrett. 2018. *Patients Come Second: Leading Change by Changing the Way You Lead*. New York: Inc. Original.

Index

Note: Italicized page locators refer to exhibits.

Communication strategy: comprehensive, consistent, and pervasive, 105
Community care: post-COVID-19 reality and, 5
Communityship: spreading through the organization, 102
Compassion, 12; as core value at Mayo Clinic, 35
Competition: in payment environment, 20
Complex: in VUCA (volatile, uncertain, complex, and ambiguous) dynamics, 8
Conformity: in Schwartz's ten universal values, 31, *31*
Consistency, 93; trust and, 59, 61
Control, 47; meaningful work and sense of, 50; in progression from professional to manager to leader, 115–16, *116*
Core values: specifically defining for healthcare organizations, 35–36; successful healthcare organizations and, 66. *See also* Corporate values
Corporate culture: alignment of personal and corporate values in, 12, 36, 43, 50–51, 65, 70, 78, 83, 99, 105, 117, *130*, 130–35, 145, 147, 170; of American College of Healthcare Executives, 100, *101*; breach of, 103–4; financial performance and, 102–3, *103*; foundations of, 99, *100*, 106, 110; key elements of, 10, *11*; Level 5 leaders and, 117–18; as "organization's personality," 97–98, 109; six elements of, 101; at Spectrum Health, 107–9, *109*; strengthening, leadership communication for, 105–7; strong, organizational values and, 32; understanding and importance of, 97–99; values alignment and, 36; vibrant and strong, 41
Corporate tangibles and intangibles: of healthcare delivery systems, 9, 9–10, 45–47, *46*
Corporate values: alignment with personal values, 12, 36, 43, 50–51, 65,

70, 78, 83, 99, 105, 117, *130*, 130–35, 145, 147, 170; core, corporations driven by, 13–14
Corporate vision statements: examples of, 53–54
Covey, Stephen R., 55, 127
COVID-19 pandemic, 16, 56, 57, 60, 118, 120, 143; Dartmouth-Hitchcock Medical Center during, 176; employee engagement at Scripps Health System during, 77–78; employee engagement issues and, 124; healthcare workers and purpose during, 71; human costs of, 173; lifelong learning focus in wake of, 134; Maslow's hierarchy of needs and providers during, 84; power of trust and, 59; relationships and impact of, 72; Spectrum Health providers during, 107–8; universal commitment of healthcare providers during, 169; unprecedented challenge for leaders during, 120; values of healthcare providers and response to, 26–27; VUCA (volatile, uncertain, complex, and ambiguous) world and, 4, 21
Crain's Detroit Business's 2019 "Health Care Heroes," 107
Cross-cultural understanding, 75
Csikszentmihalyi, Mihaly, 50, 137
Cultural accommodation, 36–37
Cultural anthropology, 36
Cultural norms, 99
Culture, 47; anthropological, 36, 98, 99; defining, 97, 98, 99–105; healthcare, 37–41; as the "organization's personality," 97–98, 109; strategy *vs.*, 99; strength of, *100*. *See also* Corporate culture; Organizational culture
Culture-building communication, 106
Customer satisfaction, 47, 178
Cynics: contribution to performance, *149*, 150, 151, 152; replacing, 156

"Healthcare heroes" of the pandemic: values and, 27
Healthcare industry: current dynamics of, 1–3; uncertainty and change in, 118
Healthcare organizations: "right" and "wrong" people for, 148–52, *149*; successful, three key components in, 66
Healthy organizations: sustainable employee engagement and, 173
Hedonism: in Schwartz's ten universal values, 31, *31*
Herzberg, Frederick, 85
Heskett, James, 102
Hidden agendas: trust issues and, 58, 59
Hierarchy of needs (Maslow), 29–30, *30*, 84
Highly capable individuals: in Collins's leadership hierarchy, *116*
High performers: reinforcing, 89–90
High-performing organizations: corporate culture of, six elements in, 101; with engaged employees and genuine leaders, 170; meaningful work in, 48; traits of, *171*
Hiring: hire to fit, not to fill, 132; values alignment and, 50
Home building: visioning process in, 53
Honesty, 93, 174, 175; trust and, 59, 61
Hospitals: Peter Drucker on, 8; VUCA (volatile, uncertain, complex, and ambiguous) dynamics and, 5
Hsieh, Tony, 97
Hubris, 157
Hudelson, Patricia M., 98
Human resources management, 143
Human systems: reinforcing clarity through, 165, 167
Humility, 117, 127
Husel, William, 104
"Hyper-verbal" communication: new teams and, 142

Iacocca, Lee, 163
Ideological/political values, 13
Individualism: physicians and, 40

Individual professional development plan, 134
Influence: leadership process and, 114, 126; in progression from professional to manager to leader, 115–16, *116*
Innovation: as core value at Mayo Clinic, 35
Inpatient care, 5
Inputs: tangible/intangible aspects of healthcare delivery systems and, *9*, 10, *46, 47*
Integrated health care delivery systems: post-COVID-19 reality and, 5
Integrity: as core value at Mayo Clinic, 35
Intellect: emotional intelligence and, 75
Intensive care units: filled, COVID patients and, 120
Intermediate care centers, 5
Internal motivation: money, sustainable performance, and, 89
International Journal for Quality in Healthcare, 98
Internet, 169
Interpersonal intelligence, 73
Interviewing and selection: values alignment and, 50, 131–32, 145, 147
Intrapersonal intelligence, 74
Intrinsic motivation: personal investment and, 86; self-sustaining nature of, 94
iPhone, 169

Job crafting, 67
Jobs, Steve, 1, 129
Job satisfaction: sustainable, 85
Johns Hopkins University School of Medicine, 2
John Templeton Foundation: on psychology of purpose, 66
Joy, 71, 72
Judgmental listening, 141

Kaiser Family Foundation, 72
Kaplan, Alan, 70, 123–25
Kirsch, Michael, 2
Koch brothers, 165
Kotter, John, 102, 151
Kramer, Steven, 47

Mead, Margaret, 36
Meaning, 117, 119; alignment of personal and corporate values and, 15; as element of happiness, 71, 72; flow and, 50; meaning of, 45–61; personal values and, 14; positive psychology and, 71; research on, 49–51; in work, importance of, 45–49; in work, values and, 27
Meaning and purpose model, 8–12; components of, 12–18; corporate values and, 13–14; meaning and, 14–15; mission/vision and, 15–17; personal values and, 12–13; purpose and, 17–18; sequential elements in and implementation of, 12, 18, 147, 170
Meaningful life: happiness and, 71
Meaningful work: factors related to, 28; as a function of organizational vision, *130*, 135–36, 145; leadership application, 51–54; purpose and, 117; trust as bridge from vision to, 55–59
"Meaning in life" notion: definition of, 14
Medical errors: systemic problems and, 2
Medscape National Burnout and Suicide Report, 1
Mentors and mentoring, 133, 174
Mergers and acquisitions, 137
Merritt Hawkins, 3
Methodist Health System (Indiana), 143
Meyer, Kurt, 143–44
Mihaljevic, Tomislav: on post-COVID-19 reality and caregiving, 4–5
Millennials, 118; generational communication and, 176; professional development and, 134
Miller, Kim, 69, 173, 174–75
Mintzberg, Henry, 102
Mission, 20, 21, 78, 178; connection to greater purpose and, 65–66, 170; corporate culture built on foundation of, 99, *100*, 106, 110; definition of, 16; finding purpose in, *130*, 137–38; finding purpose in work and, 67–73; organization's "soul" and, 145; at Spectrum

Health, 108, *109*; strong corporate cultures anchored by, 37; sustainable employee engagement and, 117; for Utopia Health (fictional case study), 163; values creating meaning in work and, 27, *28. See also* Values; Vision
Mission–purpose: creating corporate culture based on, 10, *11*; sustainable employee engagement and, 8
Mission statement, 16, 137, 169; as corporate charter, 100; organization's "reason for being" in, 66; for selected healthcare organizations, examples of, 68–70; successful healthcare organizations and, 66; vision statement *vs.,* 67
Mission statement test: passing, 68
Mission/vision: in employee engagement model, 15–17
Modern Healthcare "Top Women Leaders" list, 107
Money: as a demotivator, 82, 87; employee development *vs.,* 90; as a motivator, limits of, 48–49, 94; as a motivator: myths and realities, 87–90
Moon landing: mission/vision and, 16
Morale: low, personal intangibles and, 10; universal erosion of, in a VUCA (volatile, uncertain, complex, and ambiguous) world, 3
Motivation, 75; common theories of, 83–87; complex nature of, 93; definition of, 83; employee, unleashing, 81–82; extrinsic or external, 87, 94; in gambling, 88; intrinsic or internal, 86, 89, 94; levels of, 15; misconceptions about, 81, 82, 93; personal values aligned with organizational values and, 33–34
Motivational drivers, 86–87
Motivation Factor: A Theory of Personal Investment (Maehr and Braskamp), 86
Motivation-hygiene theory (Herzberg), 85–86
Motivation maintenance: in Herzberg's motivation-hygiene theory, 86

Racism: systemic, combating, 29
Raphael, Daniel, 12
Rashid Al Maktoum, Mohammed bin, 165
Receiver: talking in the language of, 140
Recognition: challenge coins and, 92, *93*; drive for, 86, 87
Recruitment: values alignment and, 50, 130, 131, 147
Reflective listening, 57, 141
Reflexive behaviors, 36
Relationship management, 74
Relationships: building, 114, 125, 126; as element of happiness, 71, 72
Religious beliefs and values, 12, 13
Re-recruitment: of stars, 152, 153; values alignment and, 131, 134–35, 147
Research: post-COVID-19 reality and funding of, 5
Resilience, 174
Resistance to change myth, 121, 126
Respect: as core value at Mayo Clinic, 34; team members at Baptist Medical Center and, 91–92
Retirement: of baby boom generation, 118
Retirement planning: personal, examples of, 53; vision elements in, 136
Robotics, 168, 177
Rogers, Will, 129
Role clarification: vision discussions and, 107

Safety needs: in Maslow's hierarchy of needs, 30, *30*
Salaries: competitive, 89
Satisfiers: in Herzberg's motivation-hygiene theory, 85
Schaninger, Bill, 49, 50
Schein, Edgar, 97
Schultz, Howard, 65
Schwartz, Shalom H.: ten universal values theory, 30–32, *31*
Scripps Health System (La Jolla, California): Chris Van Gorder's leadership of, 76; mission and vision statements of, 68–69; vision statement of, 54

Security: in Schwartz's ten universal values, 31, *31*
Selective and judgmental listening, 56, 57
Self-actualization: in Maslow's hierarchy of needs, 30, *30*
Self-assessment, 170
Self-awareness, 74
Self-confidence, 75
Self-direction: in Schwartz's ten universal values, 31, *31*
Self-knowledge, 76
Self-management, 74, 76
Self-regulation, 74
Seligman, Martin, 70, 71
Senior executives: organizational change and, 121; vision statement and, 51, 52
Sense of self: value differences between physicians *vs.* executives and, *38,* 40
Servant leadership, 76
"Seven Innate Human Values: The Basis for Consistent Ethical Decision-Making" (Raphael), 12
Shareholders: higher-performing cultures and 3× return to, 101; maximizing return of, 34
"Sick care" system: Brian Silverstein on, 19
Silva, Alberto, 114
Silverstein, Brian, 18–19
Situational leadership, 114
Skeptics: contribution to performance, *149,* 150, 151, 152
Skinner, B. F., 84, 85, 87, 88
Slishman, Sam, 2
Slogan: vision *vs.,* 53
"Slow no": physicians *vs.* executives and, 39
Slugs: contribution to performance, *149,* 150, 151–52; replacing, 156
Smith, John: as antithesis of the employee engagement model, 156–60, 161
Social awareness, 74
Social change: value-based perceptions and, 29
Social data, 5
Social management skills, 76
Social norms: values and, 12

About the Author

Tom Atchison, EdD, is president and founder of Atchison Consulting LLC. Since 1984, Dr. Atchison has consulted with healthcare organizations on managed-change programs, team building, and leadership development. He presents to thousands of healthcare professionals every year on the elements of effective organizations. He has written and been featured in numerous articles and broadcasts about motivation, managed change, team building, and leadership.